Acts of Seeing

Artists, scientists and the History of the Visual
A volume dedicated to Martin Kemp

Artakt – Zidane Press

First published in 2009
by Artakt & Zidane Press

Artakt
Central Saint Martins College of Art & Design
Southampton Row, London, WC1B 4AP
www.artakt.co.uk

Zidane Press
25b Shaftesbury Road,
London, N19 4QW
www.zidanepress.com

© Artakt, Central Saint Martins College of
Art & Design, University of the Arts, London,
Zidane Press, the artists and the authors.

ISBN 97809554850–8–4

Design by Julie Hill
www.juliehill.co.uk

Cover illustration: *Lens*, Claude Heath, 2006,
122 x 66 cm. © The Artist.
www.claudeheath.com

With thanks to Olga and Pieter Dreesmann,
and Gheri Sackler for their generous support.

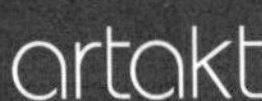
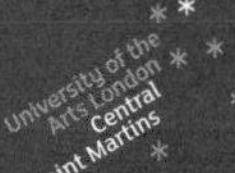
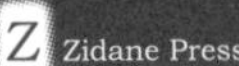

Acts of Seeing

Artists, scientists and the History of the Visual
A volume dedicated to Martin Kemp

Edited by Assimina Kaniari & Marina Wallace

Contents

Foreword

'Eyeballing' – the act of seeing – and the business of writing about it
There is always a fresh sense of urgency in Martin Kemp's published writings. He keeps most of the information alive in his mind, and accesses it selectively and creatively as his thinking develops, adding wide-ranging references as he proceeds with his research. He writes quickly, generally in not much more than one or two drafts, and the immediacy of his writing style is infectious and memorable. Furthermore, his more spontaneous writings, unpublished or never-intended-to-be-published, are positively exciting and surprising. The thrill of looking at his unpublished notes is similar to that of undertaking a rich treasure hunt.

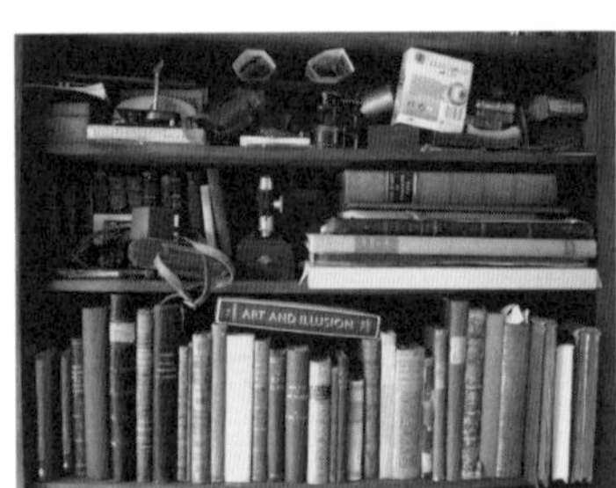 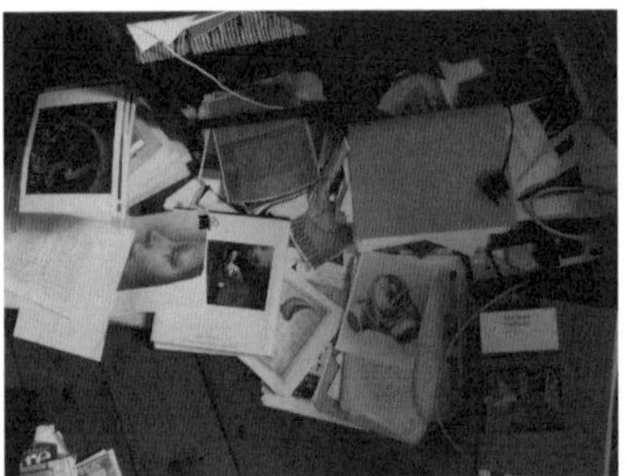

FIGURE 1 and 2 Martin Kemp's study, Woodstock, Oxford, 1999.

I was lucky to be able to go through Martin's papers on and under the shelves of his study in his house in Woodstock, near Oxford. Piles and piles of written material stack up in every corner, and each one speaks of the job in hand. My preferred piles are those with sketched-out notes and diagrams, rough hand-written annotations, and my favourite pile of all is that of Martin's lively correspondence with David Hockney. Some of it was published in *Secret Knowledge* (Thames & Hudson, 2001).

Some, going back to 1998, still lies under Martin's desk, in a large box filled with exciting documentation including David's faxes and Martin's responses, postcards, photocopies of pages from art history books illustrating paintings and drawings, and other kinds of memorabilia relevant to David's book on optical devices and their usage in art throughout the centuries. On one page, in response to David's faxed paper, Martin writes:

> *I think it is tremendously important and exciting that an artist who has spent a lifetime (sorry, sounds posthumous!) translating the seen scene into painting, with all the intensity of eyeballing and experiment that is involved, is subjecting the 'old masters' to radical scrutiny.*

The term 'eyeballing' (originally David Hockney's invention) is typical of Martin Kemp's vocabulary, a vocabulary which is down-to-earth and yet precise, shifting meaning whilst, at the same time, describing. The confidence displayed in his writing is reflected in a playful and creative oscillation between specialized and common language. In his introduction to his book, *Seen | Unseen* (Oxford, 2006) Martin writes of specialization:

> *Someone who inhabits any territory of specialized knowledge will inevitably and properly entertain opinions on matters at lesser or greater degrees of remove from that territory. A bricklayer has as much right to express deeply held views about goodness or venality of his or her fellow human beings as the most erudite of moral philosophers. The philosopher should be able to draw on a range of references and articulate arguments about what is considered good in a way that the bricklayer could not and would not need to do. The apparent academic superiority of an academic's philosophical discourse over the robust assertion of a worker in the building trade does not mean that the latter cannot pose a challenge to the former. A hands-on worker may address something from a practical perspective which the most sophisticated philosopher can ignore only at his or her peril.*

Another frequent expression used in Kemp language is 'looking like.'

> *By talking of what something 'looks like,' I am not referring to the image on the retina of the eye, or even to some kind of image compounded in our brain as a kind of 'photo-*

graph' of what is out there. What I am talking about is the collective result of an incred-
ibly complex interaction between the buzzing confusion of visual stimuli, the optics of
seeing, the neuro-physics of sensation, the cognitive systems that come into play, and
the huge baggage of experience, knowledge, assumption, context, and directed interest
that sets structured parameters on how we operate the processes of determining what
something 'looks like.' (Seen | Unseen, p.79)

Complexity is not a daunting concept in 'Kempian' thought as it comes infused with helpfully wide-ranging references that expand the limits of complex thought in a friendly and easily accessible way. With what he calls *'semiotic crochet work,'* Kemp criticises an almost intentionally obtuse use of language that potentially snowballs in an exclusive and closed discourse. ¶ On the 17th of October 1999, in another hand-written letter to David Hockney, the busy and reflective art historian address-es the searching great living artist, siding with him, and refers to the great dead artist, Leonardo:

Dear David,

Finally, Sunday evening, some relenting of commitments and a chance to respond. I
hope you got my musings of the Raphaelite/Cezanne see-saw.

Did you see the Spanish still life (almost wrote 'stiff life') show at the National Gal-
lery, London, a few years ago? Very impressive – a revelation. I knew Zurbaran, the
extraordinary super-presence of a few discrete objects lit (as it were) from within. But
Sánchez Cotán (early) and Meléndez (late) were eye-openers for an eye-baller. Yes,
it's not 'stiff life,' or gradually 'dying life,' and not even still in the sense of lifeless
– more stilled for a moment. It's that sense that the contemplative time for the artist's
intensity of looking is in dialogue with a particular moment of the existence of an or-
ganic, perishable thing. That's what you have seen. I know absolutely what you mean,
although I had never thought about it in quite that way. ¶ *It's the same dilemma*
– the perishability – that Leonardo faced in his anatomical work, particularly in the
Italian climate with no preservatives! What he wrote was: 'To you who say that it is
better to witness an anatomy than to see the drawings, you would say justly, if it were
possible to see all these things that are in such designs if they were demonstrated in

The period of correspondence with the artist was also a period of experimentation and discovery for the art historian. Whilst Hockney was trying his hand at drawing with a camera lucida, Martin and I were also looking through the optical device during excursions in Blenheim Park in Woodstock, taking breaks from reading and writing for the catalogue of the exhibition *Spectacular Bodies*. ¶ The photo overleaf (FIG 3) shows the angle of my viewing (and drawing) Martin framed by the surrounding landscape using a camera lucida. Today a few small sketchy watercolours are still leaning against the windowsills of the house in Woodstock (FIG 4). The act of seeing, for Martin, is always accompanied by the business of writing about it, and the more formal writing by more personal words, not poetry, but 'formatted prose,' as he calls it. Below is one example, unpublished, of course, and strongly linked to the published work in its pervasive emphasis on the act of seeing in Blenheim, through historical layers, up and down the commemorative monument to the Duke of Marlborough, through levels of varied knowledge, personal perceptions, natural phenomena, animal and human signs, and, above all, optical joys.

Blenheim

Sunday evening, velvet darkness subsuming a bright gem of a day.

A cold, sharp start, a sparkle of frost across ground and roofs.

Glassy ice across the puddles, shining with stilled ghosts of yesterday's ripples.

Walking in the gleaming park, the angled sun shaping hills and rugged trunks into tactile relief,

The breeze cleansing and refreshing, vitalizing the slow blood of a night's deep sleep.

Murmurs of geese, placid on the mirrored waters.

Nervous cries of pheasants, premonitions of their coming slaughter by bumping guns.

The cold Roman Duke, loftily arrogant on his soaring column, an imperial warrior out of time and place.

Nature, humanely aided, asserting its pictorial variousness. Against the geometrical bombast of the arrow-straight avenue down which he thrusts his rigid marble knee.

An English microcosm; a macrocosm of Englishness.

Muffled self-gloriousness, historically sharp, presently obscure.

With this book I would personally like to mark the great contribution that Martin has made and continues to make to the formal and informal business of looking and seeing, but also to the field of intuition, through sensing and understanding.　¶　These are acts that involve us all.

Marina Wallace

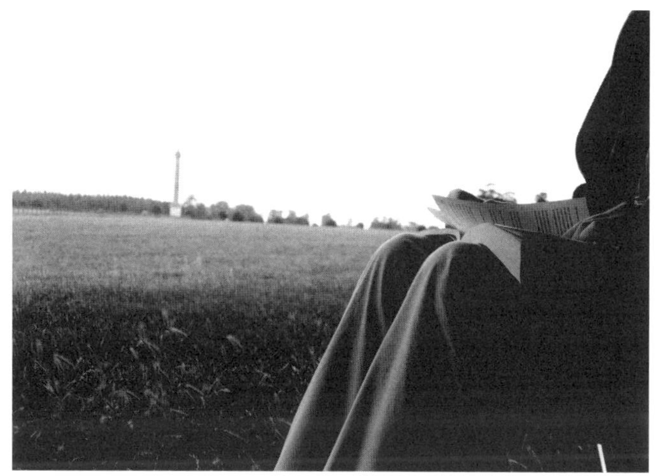

FIGURE 3 Blenheim Park, Woodstock Oxford, 1999.

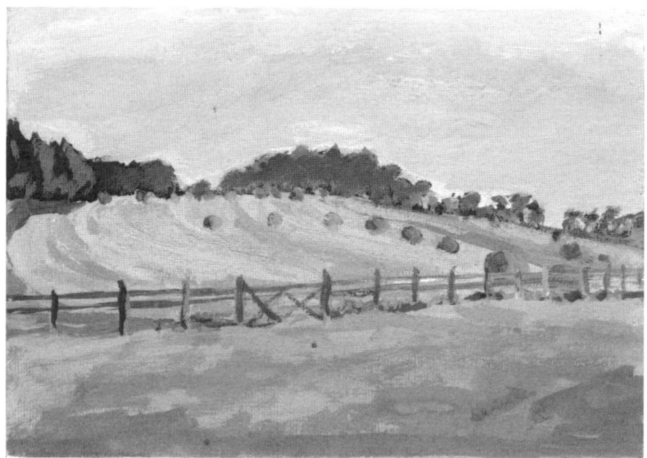

FIGURE 4 Blenheim Park, Woodstock Oxford, 1999.

Introduction

Act I *

Acts of Seeing

This book is in homage to Martin Kemp, his special and unconventional ways of looking at the world and speaking about it, his contribution to art history and the history of the visual, his continued engagement with theorists and practitioners, not to mention students of all walks of life across the many years of his academic career. *Acts of Seeing* was conceived at the time when Prof Kemp formally 'retired' from Oxford University in 2008. 'Retirement' is a strange concept for Martin Kemp. Anyone who knows him well is aware that, for such an active person, the term 're-tirement' is anacronistic. Even during the time of a very serious bout of meningitis, in 1989, he continued, from his hospital bed, to monitor the final stages of the wonderful Leonardo exhibition he curated at the Hayward Gallery, he carried on performing his duties as Chair of the Association of Art Historians, and, simultane-ously proceeded to clamorously resign, on a point of principle, from the Board of Trustees of the Victoria & Albert Museum, giving interviews to journalists visiting him in the intensive care unit clad in antiseptic masks and gowns. ¶ The essays and visual contributions dedicated to Martin Kemp in this volume are by some of the scholars and practitioners who have benefited from knowing him and exchang-ing views with him. Selecting the 'friends of Martin Kemp' has not been easy. We could have included many more, but, as always, practical imperatives dictated what we did and how we did it. This does not mean that we are not aware of many more individuals who could have added their contributions, and we thank all those who did and those who discussed the possibility with us. ¶ We are sure that there will be other occasions when those who did not write this time will in future.

Act II**

A book as an exploded view of a concept: Martin Kemp's structural intuitions and a few acts of seeing

The attention to visual structures has been a key theme in Martin Kemp's work. This has led to his interest in historiographic constructs, which in his later work explicitly take the shape of a theoretical concept coined to discuss connections between art and science on a historical and philosophical basis: the idea of 'structural intuitions.' ¶ *Acts of seeing* is a title coined by Martin Kemp to describe a collection of essays assembled by artists, theorists, historians, engineers and scientists on the theme of structural intuitions a very dear technique in Martin Kemp's cross cultural comparisons between art and science. This book is dedicated to Martin Kemp and was conceived as a thought experiment: if structural intuitions could have a life of their own beyond Martin Kemp's writing, the book in its rich conceptual and visual undertones might be taken as an exploded view of this concept. ¶ In parallel to Kemp's interest in contemporary scientists' and artists' work, one may find amongst Kemp's published work as a consistent and persistent theme, the historical exploration of the possibilities of perceived and represented structures and patterns as organisational imperatives in nature and cognition. Structures in the context of Kemp's writing not only relate to the privileged observation sites in modern science but also act most importantly as instruments for an art history of contextually examined yet philosophically approached continuities and affinities. ¶ Kemp's inquiries in the 'structural intuitions' shared by artists and scientists is a working hypothesis for an inquiry into the connections between art and science, not only in historically defined spaces for culture and but also with regard to the current and present conceptions of reality. Kemp's approach, while consistent with the highest standards of historical method, brings, at the same time, existing methods and art historical analyses into critical focus in new territories. ¶ In looking at historical questions and issues Kemp engages closely with contemporary artists and scientists in the studio, in the lab and in society. This is a critical juncture for a historical method which opens its scope into a number of conceptually defined yet biologically and ethnographically constituted possibilities. 'Structural intuitions' concern not only the past of the visual arts, architecture, science and all the material which constitute Kemp's subject matter for a history of the visual, but also the present of art and creative invention, broadly constituted. Persistent themes are explored across time and culture as they are reconfigured to play varied roles in changing societies. Kemp's connections to a number of contemporary artists-amongst documents his 'ethnographic' eye and provides the material for a future history of art historical practice that involves deep connections between art historians, artists and scientists in the 20th and 21st centuries. ¶ Encountering artists and scientists in the art history of Martin Kemp entails following the development of a number of experimental practices which constitute the subject matter of many of Kemp's analyses in response to a fundamental question in his work: why do forms take the specific shape they do at given moments? ¶ If structures and visual patterns are Kemp's favourite forms, however, far from attesting to a structuralist or realist logic of art history or reasoning they are consistently in his work elegantly placed in the cultural and institutional contexts which give rise to them. ¶ Kemp's interest in art and science not only brings the work of 20th century artists and scientists together in the study of the history of forms and structures across art and science but places such a dialogue in its contemporary and historically specific institutional contexts. ¶ Kemp's writings on science and culture, together with his extensive curating of exhibitions on art and science documents at the same time the increasingly public turn in contemporary science, as witnessed in the many books on 'popular science.' His active engagement in processes of computer visualisation, not least with the modelling of Leonardo's ideas and pictorial space, play both to the revelation of structure and to public communication. ¶ Amongst artists, architects and engineers, Richard Wentworth, Susan Derges, Karl Grimes, Claude Heath, Kate Whiteford, Tim O'Riley, Katharine Dowson, Paul Williams and Cecil Balmond contribute images and statements in response to the various collaborations and projects undertaken with art historian Martin Kemp. ¶ Ken Arnold reflects on

Kemp's exhibition work. Marina Wallace explores her own intuitions, historical and artistic, by looking at the case of a particular painting. Assimina Kaniari considers Kemp's fascination for structures as a historical fact, linking his historiographic style to late 1960s and 70s writings on perspective and geometry. Claire Farago retraces a (counter)factual history of Riegl's impact on Australian art by way of a thought experiment and Tony Robin approaches the question of perspective and the fourth dimension in art as an exercise in both creativity as well as historical method. ¶ Sir Harry Kroto discusses novel structures in science and nature from the perspective of modern chemistry while Pietro Marani sees the history of collecting in a Leonardo drawing. Katerina Reed-Tsocha ponders on Martin Kemp's philosophical style and Matt Landrus rethinks the question of beauty with regard to Leonardo's writings. Matt Gatton takes the Hockney hypothesis one step further with his palaeocamera hypothesis and Marta DeMenezes offers an account of her work on bio-art. ¶ Finally Martin Kemp's own comments to the above contributions offer a precious response both reflexive and introspective to the art of art history and its social, literary and visual boundaries.

* Marina Wallace
** Assimina Kaniari

Part I - Essays

Ken Arnold

Show business: exhibitions and the making of knowledge

A small selection of 18th century Dutch paintings, each introducing a formal group of serious gentlemen, some seemingly a little uncomfortable in their starched ruffs: these were the three or four formal, almost austere exhibits that greeted audiences to *Spectacular Bodies*. Gesturing at what was to follow, each painting also depicted some carefully rendered tropes of their profession: books and charts; a skull, tibia or fully articulated skeleton; a wax head and neck, or some anatomical specimen. Effectively serving as the exhibition's hosts, here was an assured company of medical men prepared to let us into the extraordinary world of their inner knowledge. It was an impressive, if understated, start to a breathtakingly bold exhibition.   ¶   Next came an artfully arranged showcase of some half dozen or so surgical implements – some Ravens' Hook forceps, a wrought iron amputation saw, and other humble, though somewhat menacing, tools of their trade. And then, walking up the long ramp from the Hayward Gallery's ground floor, visitors were greeted with a truly unforgettable hall of images and sculptures of flayed bodies, mostly delicate visual explorations of the material lurking beneath human skin. This theatre of anatomical insights strongly evoked the didactic spaces that had been set up from the Renaissance on, where students and the casually curious gathered in order to peruse scientific displays and performances. The final ingredients stirred into the startling display of medicine's exuberant past were judiciously chosen works of contemporary art: Marc Quinn's frozen plant flesh, suspended in time, and John Isaacs' disturbing wax rendering of the anatomised human form as a messy piece of meat, spattered with blood. By turns dramatic and chilling; beautiful, informing and intriguing, *Spectacular Bodies* lived up to its proud title, representing a landmark exhibition. It was a show overseen by a curatorial team prepared to 'think aloud,' to break disciplinary rules for good historical and aesthetic reasons: an exercise in visual investigation that unambiguously added to what we know about the world. ¶ For many of us lucky enough to see it, Martin Kemp and Marina Wallace's exhibition has become lodged as a profoundly memorable gallery experience, an exemplar of contemporary ideas-led curating at its very best. For Kemp, it followed a number of other remarkable shows, most notably his 1989 *Leonardo da Vinci. Artist, Scientist, Inventor,* again at the Hayward Gallery in London, and in 1992 a collaborative venture entitled *Circa 1492: Art in the Age of Discovery* mounted at the National Gallery in Washington D C. In each, he showed that a scholar at the top of his academic career was willing and able to use the public medium of exhibitions to think through visual and material culture in a rather different fashion. ¶ The inspiration derived from seeing *Spectacular Bodies* and a few other heady thematic shows, combined with my own involvement in a number of exhibition projects with the Wellcome Trust, has encouraged me to begin investigating a number of questions about the role of exhibitions and events within public culture. What is the nature of the curatorial process, and at its core the investigative habits and the intellectual temper of those who undertake it? What are the fundamental characteristics of the spaces in which exhibitions happen and what role do visitors themselves play while they stroll through them. What types of things are put on display and what register, what impact do they have? And emerging from these incremental, more practical questions, I am fundamentally interested in the sort of knowledge, if any, that is created through exhibitions. Given how much recent analysis there has been of museums, galleries and their histories, it is surprising how little serious attention has been paid to the cultural significance of temporary exhibitions and events. To pursue these interests, I have therefore set about interviewing influential professionals working in the area. One of the first people I wanted to talk to was Martin Kemp. So on the afternoon of 28 March 2008 we met up at Trinity College, Oxford, to discuss these topics. We sat at a large table with just a recorder and Martin's hat between us. We talked and talked while dusk drew in, the room becoming almost dark by the time we finished. The following essay takes as its starting point that conversation.

Magicians with strange goods

I am interested then in the creative habits involved and epistemological significance of taking exhibits out of storeroom cupboards and drawers and assembling them in public displays. These practices are in fact as old as the modern museum itself. As Andrea Phillips has pointed out, it is an idea that was already evident in the efforts of very early museum 'show-men' like the John Tradescants, who in the 17th century set up England's first museum in Lambeth. They were, she asserts, 'self-made magician[s]: the tale-teller[s], the money-spinner[s], the alchemist[s] of objects transposed from one route to another.' Like their 'ark' (the name given to the Tradescant cabinet), the more contemporary projects I am also interested in, provide the public with 'the chance to witness a perverse hiatus in the movement of strange goods from one place to another; a moment of pause, in which the mobility of objects came to unnatural stature.'   ¶   Curators have always acted as magicians licensed to conjure and spin tales out of strange goods. But what makes them good at this? What are their key skills? Intriguingly, when questioned, Martin Kemp seems not immediately to think of himself as a curator at all. And he is definitely not keen to think of himself as a curator-author, who just happens to be working in a different medium. Too often, he says, that metaphor leads to exhibitions in which the star curator 'somehow becomes the main exhibit.' Instead, he is more interested in the notion of exhibitions emerging from a collective, integrated activity across many different components and professional callings: design, education, conservation, communications, construction and so forth. Better then, insists Kemp, to look to musical ensembles or sports teams for comparable creative groupings. 'I'm very interested, [he says], in how you get the diverse strengths of people [in a sports team] meshing and operating really well ... the great skill is not to play to somebody's weaknesses but to identify within your team what the people are good at, and play to those strengths. And get the total effect bigger than just if the people are working individually.' Curators, Kemp implies, have to be as much concerned with conducting public performances as with pursuing scholarly research, and maybe precisely with the job of making the two meaningfully converge.[1]   ¶   The etymology of the word reveals that the curatorial role is a caring one – keepers who were initially charged to act as shepherds protecting parts of institutional collections. What exhibition curators have done is effectively to extend (and maybe partially convert) that protective role further to cover the somewhat more unruly gallery offspring of temporary exhibitions, in which things are deliberately re-presented in order to become or at least suggest something else.[2] Working with the mystical aura blessed upon objects (increasingly objects drawn from ordinary life, science and technology, as well as art) once they have been transported over the threshold of a museum, exhibition curators initially seek out elements of material and visual culture that most potently and poignantly evoke a subject or topic, a problem or thesis. Obvious though it might seem, the job-defining activity of selecting telling exhibits – of understanding where to seek them out, of isolating and identifying the best amongst all the possibilities and then of knowing how to persuade individuals and institutions to let them go on show for a while – should not be glossed over lightly. Having an intuitive sense of what things will show well is a precious and surprisingly rare skill. However, it is in combination and through the connections that juxtapositions of things can suggest that exhibitions can really come into their own in exploring themes and topics – suggesting new and surprising meanings. Kemp talks about this practice as one of 'getting real things together to talk to each other.' Selecting the right exhibits and orchestrating the chatter between them is the primary means curators have to inform and shape visual knowledge.   ¶   If the role of exhibition curators has been under-analysed, the same cannot be said of artist-curators. It is a rare artist these days who does not seemingly aspire to curating at least one or two exhibitions. However, this is far from a new-minted phenomenon. A key figure in the early development of the role was the Swiss-born Harald Szeemann (1933–2005), who has been credited with inventing the job of curator at large. He came to prominence in 1969 with a landmark show: *When attitudes become form: works, concepts, processes, situations, information*, going on to a highly applauded career as a freelance curator. For Szeemann, exhibitions provided a medium of expression rather than merely a space in which to mediate art. His great ability, as his biographer Hans-Joachin Müller puts it, lay in his 'sovereign sensitivity for place, space, and local circumstance. This is what allowed him to give audiences innovative and exhilarating experiences ... [H]is greatest legacy, [Müller goes on, has been] to provide an inspiring figure for a more playful, passionate and inquisitive approach to making exhibitions.'[3] ¶ Invented (or at least boosted) in the world of contemporary art, the idea of curating an exhibition as a process of drawing specially charged things together, rather than the traditional museum role of caring for collections, has now seeped far and wide in contemporary culture. D J's, journalists, programmers, musicians and bloggers are all fundamentally curators. The audacity and playfulness of art curators like Szeemann has significantly influenced exhibition makers across dozens of disciplines, all of whom set about investigating the world through curatorial processes.[4] As a consequence, the role of the curator has moved on from merely shaping aesthetic taste to using a public platform to forge new ideas. Within this emerging professional arena an elite, almost presidential, class of übercurators (a term reflecting their frequent origin in German-speaking countries) has emerged to further exercise considerable influence on curatorial practice. Amongst the most prominent of them is Hans Ulrich Obrist, a champion of practitioners who use exhibitions as 'exploratory spaces' in which to contribute to knowledge, often making a virtue of exploiting places where one would least anticipate finding art.[5] ¶ Drawing on 'an expanded notion of art' elaborated in the 60s and 70s, Obrist has set about redefining the field: 'curating at large [as he terms it], where there would be curating of art, curating of science, curating of architecture.' So for example, an early project he undertook involved introducing an 'exhibit in[to] all the airplanes of an airline,' so that for a while Austrian Airlines featured a mobile exhibition spread across all the planes in their fleet. (It would be interesting to know if anyone actually saw the whole show). Another project involved the French artist Christian Boltanski and Fischli/Weiss, who created an exhibition in Obrist's kitchen, one deliberately not trapped by being 'about' food or cooking. Then in 1999 he extended his curatorial attention to the world of science in a project entitled *Laboratorium*, which investigated how studios and labs are more and more inter-

related, particularly in their roles as 'places where knowledge and culture are made.'
As a form of artistic practice then, this is very much the art of wondering 'what if'
– an art of imagining new ideas and of thinking in new ways about familiar ideas.
Influential far beyond the narrow world of contemporary art, the practice of those
like Obrist, has insistently put the idea of public experimentation at the heart of
modern curation.[6]

A Gripping Stroll

Exhibition curators forge ideas by experimenting with the connections between
things and novel ideas in public places. They invariably ply their craft in three dimensions, and a self-conscious awareness of the space of an exhibition is absolutely
crucial to their effectiveness. For galleries do so much more than merely house
shows. They add colour and character, of course; they decorate exhibition topics.
But they are also embedded with their own messages, meanings and ideas, inevitably adding their own voice. Even without formal architectural or design training,
curators need to pay careful attention to the nature of the floors, ceilings and walls
of exhibition halls, to the lighting, to the plinths, text panels, labels and so forth.
Professionally speaking, however, it tends to be designers who are responsible for
the visual setting of a show. Consequently, as Martin Kemp points out, the moment
when designers get involved in an exhibition has a strong bearing on the visitors'
physical experiences of it. Kemp recommends their early involvement, rather than
getting them 'to design an exhibition which has [already] been conceived ... [making
sure the designer] is part of the conceptual framing of it.'   ¶   Surprisingly maybe,
the role of the designer in articulating the idea of an exhibition has received somewhat more analysis than that of the curator. A focus on the visitors' experiences
led, from the 1930s on, to a particular concern with how effective communications
could emerge from the collaborative effort of curators and designers in bonding the
story and its look. As an example, historian Charlotte Klonk has shown how early
20th century German designers (working both in museum and commercial settings)
applied themselves to the task of engaging visitors first by visually attracting their

attention, and then by providing a 'pleasant stroll,' relating exhibits or objects one to another and imparting information with impact. The critic of the time, Karl Scheffler summed up the core understanding that enabled them to do this as 'the fundamental laws of bodily feeling and [how to] articulate them in space.'[7] ¶ Early analysis of the exhibition experience assumed the model of a passive audience being led along from one node of information to another. More recently, however, most museum researchers have instead adopted a different view in which visitors have become active participants in their own experiences, 'collaborating' with the exhibition makers in how the spaces are negotiated and how meaning is extracted from them. And as Martin Kemp insists, their self-constructed experience of the show starts at its threshold. Paul Williams, Kemp's favoured exhibition designer, insists on providing an initial quiet space and perhaps a single object or some other element that enables visitors mentally to shake off the frustrations of getting to the venue: a decompression chamber of sorts in which they can gain composure and embrace the exhibition itself. ¶ Once over this threshold and thoroughly within the exhibition, arguably the most important element of designing/curating the visitor experience lies in the art of juxtaposition – that is in creating the gaps and pauses that articulate the physical and mental passage between one thing and another. Though blindingly obvious, it is crucial to remember that this experience of moving on is fundamentally ambulatory, albeit in the rather unusual conditions of relative darkness and at an artificially slow pace. This 'museum walk' – the tryingly controlled, cleric-like movement that visitors have to make with their feet or wheelchair wheels in order to get round an exhibition – provides the governing pace and pattern of their mental meanderings. Focussing on walking as a fundamentally cerebral experience is the great insight that Rebecca Solnit shares in her *Wanderlust: a history of walking*. The history of walking, she insists, has also to be understood as a history of thinking. And from the 18th century on, she argues, when the idea of controlling, taming and moulding the environment in order to 'stage a thought' first emerged, walking became an important part of the history of ideas – a form of constructed visual journey for the imagination, 'leisurely enough both to see and to think over the sights, to assimilate the new into the known.' And while walking 'everything stays connected.' To walk, Solnit further asserts, is to put the mind in motion at about three miles per hour. Exhibitions, it seems to me, provide a special, and especially concentrated, form of this mental movement, where the speed is dramatically slowed down to maybe closer to 0.3 miles per hour. This is the pace of an average visitors' stuttering progress and thought processes through a show: their 'investigations, rituals and meditations.' Fundamentally then, the job of the exhibition team is to choreograph a gripping stroll through one or more medium-sized rooms.[8] ¶ In practice, this concept of curatorship as an exercise in controlling the chance visual encounters of a stroller (ensuring that they have an interesting walk) was already central to early exhibition experiments by, for example, Bauhaus artist Lázló Moholy-Nagy. His 1929 display in Zehlendorf (a Berlin suburb) employed the careful placing of doors, walls and corridors, so that, as Charlotte Klonk describes it, 'the visitor [had] the feeling of a leisurely walk without losing the aim or the security of an aim from consciousness.' [40.7 p.490] This rigorous and rational approach to ordering a visitor's experience of an exhibition (as some sort of architectural performance) was described by Adolf Behne at the time as 'an organised path along a specific set of objects in a specific unequivocal direction and sequence.' [40.8 p.493] This tightly choreographed approach to exhibition making, which arguably can be traced back to Renaissance masques and before, continues today in, for example, parts of David Wilson's Museum of Jurassic Technology in Los Angeles and in the highly cinematographic exhibitions of film-maker Peter Greenaway, as well as in some rather old-fashioned didactic science exhibitions. But even here, visitors are able to exercise their own inclinations for free association and meaning-making. For all that, though the passage through the space might be overtly led and the preferred sequence of stimuli suggestively implied, the exhibits themselves, the fashion in which they are examined, and the stories embodied within them nevertheless remain irrepressibly open.

Enriched things

Exhibitions provide public spaces in which curators and designers orchestrate stimulating walks. Along the way, the key inspirational ingredient they employ are the 'enriched things' that museums and galleries store, and that in turn keep them alive. Exhibits are 'nodes,' as Lorraine Daston has them, where matter and meaning come together in the most pronounced of fashions. And in bringing materiality and meaningfulness together, museum objects embody a form of concrete rather than abstract knowledge – a knowledge without which we might, speculates Daston, even stop talking, becoming 'as mute as things are alleged to be.' Furthermore, the worldly understanding that they manifest is frequently charged with personal insights – information about a thing is often only known because it has been divulged by someone with a particular relationship to the object. Not just adding to our understanding then, these are objects that can potentially make us *feel* things. For as Sherry Turkle reminds us, we 'think with the objects we love; [and] we love the objects we think with.' The Russian's in fact have two words for things: *predmet* refers simply to functional entities, while *vesch* are furnished with an essence, a spirit even. And museums, of course, are one of the places where *predmet* can be converted into *vesch*. As objects endowed with a soul, it is the *vesch* that tend to be the most eloquent parts of a collection or exhibition.[9] ¶ These sorts of ideas have been extensively explored by philosophers, anthropologists and students of museum practice. But what researchers in these fields seem to have been less concerned with is the way that putting objects on show can influence how they are made to speak. Of course, contemporary exhibitions involve show-casing an increasingly wide range of categories of material – each with its own density of meaning and register of voice. The spectrum goes from display furniture (cradles and frames), labels and text panels, computer graphics, props, models, simulations and replicas, right through to historic artefacts from everyday life and on up to original artworks. Different curators, and indeed different curatorial projects, work with different proportions of each. Arguably, it is the internet with its promise to enable universal access to anything, anywhere and at anytime (or at least its digitised informational content) that has enabled us to re-evaluate the museum and gallery's role in providing something very different: encouraging people instead to be concerned with 'just this, just here, and just now.' For a curator like Martin Kemp, a Leonardo drawing has a visual potency that gives it the very highest register of impact. A model on the other hand 'sits there and it does a particular kind of job,' as does a piece of computer generated animation. With skill, all these elements can be presented in close relation to each other to the mutual benefit of each. So for example, a plate from Robert Hooke's pioneering book of microscopy presented alongside a working microscope and specimen, a biological model and maybe a piece of contemporary glass sculpture that plays with ideas of scale can, cumulatively, provide a highly nuanced and mutually reinforcing way of grappling with the abstract topic of the invisibly small, as well as cultural developments in how scientists, artists and others have probed it. ¶ One of the most potent curatorial habits that has been increasingly exploited in exhibitions over the last decade and a half (exemplified in shows like *Spectacular Bodies* and others that have followed in its footsteps) is the deliberate juxtaposition of objects and perspectives from science and art. Trained in Natural Sciences before taking up the study of art history, Kemp is rather well placed simultaneously to explore both spheres, enabling him to draw out their shared ways of proceeding through, as he puts it, 'observation, structured speculation, visualization, exploitation of analogy and metaphor, experimental testing, and the presentation of remade experience in particular styles.' Within this framework, he tellingly finds scientific resonances in works of art, as well as visual potency in scientific images. The 'style of scientific artefacts [he concludes] is no less integral to the communication of content and meaning than style in a work of art.' Things in science figure then as 'communicative objects within various communities – the narrowly professional, the broader worlds of science and learning, the influential audiences of patrons and founders, and various kinds of public from elite to the so-called popular.' What Kemp's own curatorial exercises show is just how much can be teased out of them from playfully juxtaposing things from these different contexts within the public sphere.[10] ¶ What these 'conversations' between science and art rely on is a confluence of different types of visual thinking that enables their objects meaningfully to interact across the same gallery floor. As James Elkins, another champion of visual thinking, points out, this approach to knowledge can be spread out still further, and certainly into almost every department on the university campus. Most 'visual work in the university [he has found], is done outside the humanities, but most of the claims to be doing visual work came from within the humanities.' 'Images are being made and discussed in dozens of fields, throughout the university and well beyond the humanities. Some fields, such as biochemistry and astronomy, are image-obsessed; others think and work *through* images.' What Elkins seems less aware of is the rich potential for new multi-disciplinary, investigation-led curatorship to respond to his call to 'pay close-grained attention to the ways people make and talk about images.' Museums and galleries may in fact be in a particularly strong position in this regard, especially since, as he is quick to point out, universities seem oddly slow to embrace a curiosity for visual knowledge, even while making and consuming so much. 'There is a large literature arguing that visuality is the pre-eminent medium of our experience of the world [says Elkins] but universities continue to pursue text-based and mathematics-based education.' Elkins' assumption seems to be that universities should now turn their attention to this visual thinking. This may well be so, but in the mean time I would contend that public temporary exhibitions are already grappling in interestingly different ways with this material, and creating from it a vibrant alternative grade of knowledge.[11]

Showing knowledge

The best temporary exhibitions are created by visual thinkers intent on forging new ideas through the juxtaposition of enriched things arranged so as to lead primed visitors on a mindful and invigorating stroll. And at their best, they unquestionably have an important role to play even in the livelihood of specific disciplines (particularly in the arts and at least some parts of the humanities), and especially in facilitating broader public engagement with them. Indeed, various essayists in a recent volume entitled *The Two Art Histories* have argued rather more forcefully for the scholarly role of exhibitions (within that specific discipline) both 'as sites of innovative art historical scholarship' and as a form of 'visual demonstration, as a discourse that functions by *showing* rather than by writing.' Thinking precisely about the nature of the ideas at stake in an exhibition, Alfred Lichtwark (a museum director in Hamburg at the turn of the twentieth century) likened the function of exhibitions to a form of essay 'serious in intent but quite loose in form ... not scholarly according to German academic standards, but merely stimulating, letting ideas be guessed at rather than expressing them directly.'[12] ¶ Exhibition curation has evolved enormously since Lichtwark's day, but the epistemological significance of a temporary show is still more allied to the generation of stimulating hunches than the academic habit of professing great certainties. As suggested above, this license for a freer flow of ideas and connections between them has been greatly exploited in curatorial projects that dare to leave behind the security of strict disciplinary boundaries, and that treat the inevitably eclectic choice and positioning of material as an extension of the contemporary artist's desire to apply new meanings to existing things. With well-chosen themes, or topics, or indeed methodologies, exhibitions have begun to play a role in actually creating knowledge (driven by a type of thinking almost impossible to imagine in the current academic sphere), rather than just disseminating pre-existing understanding. For Martin Kemp, the type of insight that exhibitions provide is rather particular, based on 'a series of visual intuitions.' Although absolutely grounded in real information – after all, footnotes in the form of framed or showcased exhibits, are there for all to see – this is an altogether different character of knowledge. It is more akin to lateral mental skips and looser, more playful insights that so frequently can lead to new uncommon forms of sense, rather than straight declarations of information or data, or arguments for hypotheses and theories. By its nature it tends to be somewhat tentatively proffered in a three dimensional space, theoretically at least, openly accessible to all the public. Less a public parade of pre-existing ideas, some temporary exhibitions instead catch knowledge in the process of becoming. ¶ In a university environment fundamentally constructed around the need to police disciplinary boundaries, the difficulties of finding a common language and shared methodology can be thoroughly burdensome. But many of these problems fall away in a more public environment, where experimentation is licensed on a temporary basis and where, as we have heard, visitors are involved as active, sometimes politicised, agents who help make a publicly relevant version of the show's meaning. Like TV and particularly radio broadcasts, exhibitions are hybrid beasts caught between knowledge creation and dissemination. The analogy with blogging is maybe also instructive here. As Sarah Boxer has pointed out in a recent *New York Review of Books* article, 'Many bloggers really don't write much at all. They are more like impresarios, curators, or editors, picking and choosing things they find online, occasionally slapping on a funny headline or adding a snarky … comment.' Exhibition curating by and large tends to be far more considered than this (after all, priceless objects end up being moved around the world as a consequence), but there is something compellingly similar about the two practices.[13] Both fundamentally involve toying with ideas and things that are generally considered for only a relatively short time, and with only a hazy, lingering after-life. This is ephemeral knowledge created as a form of ritualised pleasure in real (rather than virtual) public and civic places, where dialogue and debate is always possible, and where the final promise is something that might actually lift the spirits.

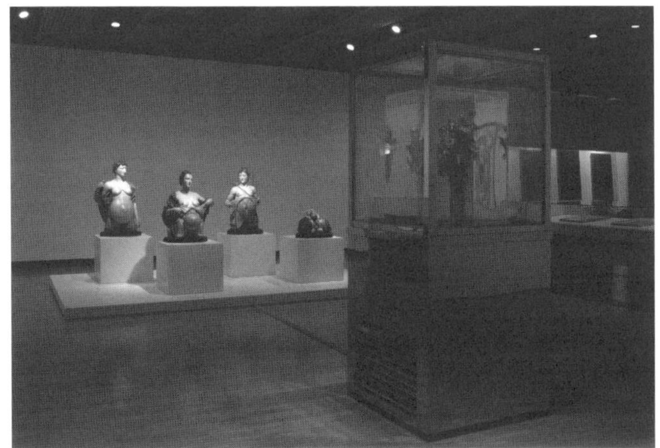

FIGURE 1 Installation shot, *Spectacular Bodies*, The Hayward Gallery, 2001–2.

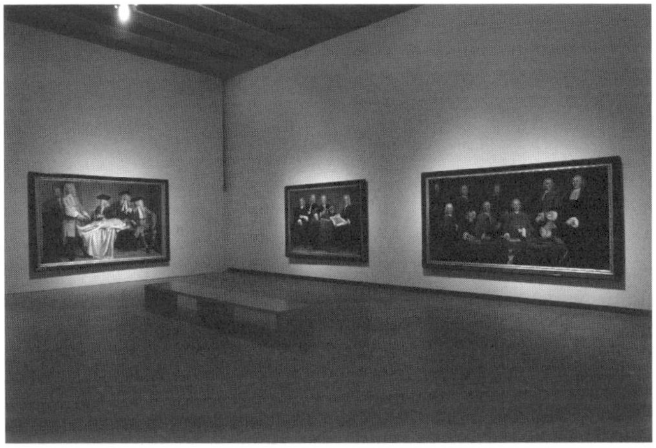

FIGURE 2 Installation shot, *Spectacular Bodies*, The Hayward Gallery, 2001–2.

1.	As Thomas Söderqvist has pointed out to me, another analogous role can be found in science in directors of research teams, where the principal investigator or head of a lab similarly leads a creative team.

2.	'Patricia Bickers, 'The Curator also Rises', *Art Monthly* 238, July/August 2000, pp.1–4. p.2.

3.	Hans-Joachin Müller, *Harald Szeemann: Exhibition maker* (Hatche Cantz Verlag, 2006) p.63.

4.	Sue Latimer, 'Artistic Licence', *Museums Journal*, Aug. 2001, pp.29–31. p.31. See too: *The Power of Display: A History of Exhibition Installations at the Museum of Modern Art*, Hardcover, (MIT, 1999). The sub-set of artist/curators that have been particularly drawn to investigating museum collections is itself a crowded one. In 1997, for example, Neil Cummings curated a show entitled *Collected*, which explored 'the depth and diversity of the collection ... from Egyptian antiquities via 18th century paintings to Marilyn Monroe memorabilia ...' Another notable project in the tradition of exhibitions exploring the idea of the museum was *The Museum of...*, comprising 'a series of temporary "museums" that ... involve[d] artists, performers, museum professionals, local residents and business people bringing this disused building to life and exploring our relationship with museums.' [Leaflet copy]. For a full survey of such projects see James Putnam, *Art and Artifact: Museum as Muse* (Thames & Hudson, 2001).

5.	Obrist has also expressed puzzlement at the 'missing literature of exhibitions.' His explanation for the gap is that 'exhibitions are not collected and that's why they fall into amnesia.' He also believes that 'we should look at curating at large, which also means unexpected curatorships – architects as curators, or scientists as curators.' [See: Paul O'Neill's interview with Hans Ulrich Obrist. (http://www.visual-culture.com/project/visual-culture/wiki/show/Pa...& www.contemporary -magazine.come/profile77_6.htm).

6.	See: 'A Rule of the game' John Brockman's discussion with Hans Ulrich Obrist, *The Third Culture* at http://www.edge.org/3rd_culture/obrist08/obrist08_index.html. Some of these ideas were also discussed at the King's Place event 'An evening with Hans Ulrich Obrist' – 23 Feb 2009.

7.	A formal professional interest in this practice has continued ever since. In 1947, an exhibition design course began at the University of Lincoln in the UK. And by the 1980s a number of museum professionals applied themselves to the question of what was the essence of what designers did and produced. (See: Geoff Matthews, 'Friendly Chimeras: The Evolution of Critical Creative Practice in *Exhibition Design* [from 'The Role of the Humanities in Design Creativity' International Conference 2007. [http://www.lincoln.ac.uk/home/conferences/human/papers/ Matthews.pdf] The Royal Ontario Museum's publication Communicating with the Museum Visitor: Guidelines for Planning (1976, Toronto, Canada: Royal Ontario Museum) proved highly influential in this area. Practitioners from the Natural History Museum in London responded with an account of their developmental psychology-inspired method for planning exhibitions in Roger Miles et al's, *The Design of Educational Exhibits* (1982, London: Unwin Hyman). Margaret Hall's different approach set out in her *On Display* (1987, London: Lund Humphries) reflected her own work at the British Museum: a 'design grammar', as she described it, focused on the task of presenting extraordinarily rich objects and collections to a broad public. For earlier European contributions to this history see Charlotte Klonk, 'Patterns of attention: from shop windows to gallery rooms in early twentieth-century Berlin' *Art History*, vol 28 no.4 September 2005, pp.468–496. p.481.

8.	Rebecca Solnit, *Wanderlust: a History of Walking* (Verso, 2001, London) pp 3-6. On the idea of 'velocities of movement' in culture, and the technological control or influence over that motion, see too Lynda Nead, *The Haunted Gallery: Painting, Photography, Film c.1900* (Yale University Press, 2008). Obrist puts this idea slightly differently as the fashioning of 'a long walk ... a sort of a "flânerie"... a promenade [in which] chance plays a very big role" ['A Rule of the game' John Brockman's discussion with Hans Ulrich Obrist, *The Third Culture* at http://www. edge.org/3rd_culture/obrist08/obrist08_index.html.

9.   *Things that Talk: Object Lessons from Art and Science* ed. Lorraine Daston (Zone Books, New York: 2004) pp.9, 16–17; *Evocative objects: things we think with* ed. Sherry Turkle (MIT Press, Cambridge, Mass, London, England: 2007) p.5, Tim Travis, 'Things with souls: The object in late Soviet culture' *Things 12*, summer 2000, pp.36–55. p38.

10. Martin Kemp, *Visualizations: the Nature book of art & science* (Oxford University Press, Oxford & N Y, 2000) pp.vi, 2, 4.

11. *Visual Practices Across the University*, ed. James Elkins. (Wilhelm Fink, München 2007) pp.7, 22, 51.

12. *The Two Art Histories: The Museum and the University*. Ed. Charles W. Haxthausen. (Stirling & Francine Clark Art Institute, Williamstown, Mass, 2002) pp. xv, xix–xx.

13. See Thomas Söderqvist, 'Museums and Blogging' at http://www.corporeality netmuseion/2008/03/23/museums-and-blogging/ and Lynn Bethke's MA thesis – 'Constructing Connections: A Museological Approach to Blogging'—from the Museology graduate program at University of Washington in Seattle (http://lynnbethke.googlepages.com/ Thesis-ConstructingConnections-absol.pdf).

Marina Wallace

The mystery of the tattered glove and the dissected knee in the anatomy lesson of Professor Röell, 1728

The Preface ...

Before delving into the content of this essay, and by way of introduction to an episode linked to the first curatorial work I did with Martin Kemp (for the exhibition *Spectacular Bodies*, Hayward Gallery, 2000–01), I should say something about the process through which I came to conceive writing the essay published here. ¶ This is inextricably linked to time spent trawling around Europe searching for artifacts to be included in the exhibition. Ken Arnold, in his essay in this volume, defines the most important part of the curatorial process aimed at designing the visitor experience, the 'art of juxtaposition – that is creating the gaps and pauses that articulate the physical and mental passage between one thing and another.' Beautifully put, and so true. In fact, the ambulatory process is not only proper of the visitor experience – walking 'around' an exhibition, as opposed to 'reading through' a book – it is also very fitting to describe part of the curator's own work. The amount of curatorial 'walking around' museum spaces, and – in the case of *Spectacular Bodies* – hospitals and anatomical repositories, is formidable. The curator moves to search for objects that will be part of the exhibition, at the time when the exhibition is still only a concept, an outline, a title with a subtitle. Not only the finished exhibition provides 'walking' material, but also the curatorial process is about walking as a way of thinking. Exhibitions, says Ken Arnold, 'provide a special, and especially concentrated, form of ... mental movement.' 'Walking around' and looking around the storage rooms of the Historisch Museum, in the periphery of Amsterdam, with chief curator Norbert Middelkoop pulling paintings out in their racks, I remember distinctly the superimposition, in my mind, of all the authoritative literature I had read about the Dutch paintings of anatomy lessons and the portraits of surgeons, including Jan Van Neck (1683), Jan Maurits Quinkhard (1732), Tibout Regters (1758), and last, but not least, Rembrandt's *Anatomy of Dr Nicolaes Tulp* (1632). 'Looking around' was of essence. ¶ What I absorbed from Martin Kemp's way of looking at the world and at his professional environment, particularly at the time of curating *Spectacular Bodies*, was what I guess Martin himself learned from Leonardo: never to be mystified by pre-existing knowledge, but rather to depend on looking attentively and discovering things for oneself. ¶ I remember one instance when, in spite of being dwarfed by Middelkoop's knowledge and expertise, I insisted on keeping out of its rack the painting by Cornelis Troost, the *Anatomy lesson of Dr Willem Röell* to continue observing the puzzling detail of the worn glove. I quizzed Martin about this, did he think it looked odd that, amidst such well attired men there should be one whose glove was torn? And what about the pointing at the well-clad knee, and the look on the man's face? Small details, but such that, as we continued looking at the painting without the expert's input, both Martin and I became increasingly intrigued by them. This puzzled state of mind led to Martin encouraging me to 'look into the matter' (or 'to look at this') in greater depth. ¶ A few months later I was ready to present the paper at an Oxford conference on anatomy and art. Norbert Middelkoop was happy with the novel interpretation now published in these pages. ¶ In the first room of the Hayward Gallery, from October 2000 to January 2001, the painting by Cornelis Troost hung next to the other Dutch anatomy lessons, conveying both its well known, and its newly acquired meaning. My pride, as curator, was both in having brought together in one single room, for the first time, the Dutch paintings of anatomy lessons (they have since been hanging together at the Amsterdam Historisch Museum) and also in having looked long and hard enough with as few preconceptions as possible, so as to reveal something quite new and surprising. To Martin I owe the habit I developed of searching for the unexpected in my curatorial activity. This is in addition to what Ken Arnold aptly calls, in a different context, the practice of the 'exercise in controlling the chance visual encounters of a stroller.' Martin himself has said that this ability is within us to start with, and that someone needs to 'open the door' to make it emerge. I am grateful to Martin for opening that door.

The essay ...

In the eighteenth century a new climate brought about and reflected some of the major changes in the tradition of group portraiture of surgeons. In his *Anatomy of Prof Petrus Camper* of 1758 Tibout Regters did away with the dissecting table and posed his sitters in a domestic interior complete with oriental carpet and imposing furniture, books and other visual references to the erudition of his subjects. Surgeons were then clearly identified with a new role as learned members of their guild, their image reminiscent of that of the governors of the guild portrayed by Nicholas Maes in 1680, and by Arnold Boonen in 1716. But it is with Cornelis Troost that we observe the birth of a new sensibility, together with some of the fundamental elements of traditional Dutch surgeons' portraiture, conveyed in an inventive and daring individual style, spiced by Troost's own particular repertoire as a painter of genre and theatre scenes. ¶ Cornelis Troost was the most important Dutch artist of the eighteenth century. In 1728, the year in which he painted *The Anatomy Lesson of Professor Röell*, his position in the Netherlands was probably not dissimilar to that of Rembrandt in 1632 (date of the *Anatomy of Dr Tulp*). For his many commissions he generally looked back to scenes of seventeenth century Dutch masters, and his satirical paintings earned him the nickname 'Dutch Hogarth.'[1] He could well have claimed, with Hogarth, that 'I have endeavoured to treat my subjects as a dramatic writer; my picture is my stage, and men and women my players, who by means of certain actions and gestures exhibit a dumb show.'[2] Troost painted scenes from theatrical performances, he was an actor himself, as well as vaguely moralising scenes. His early portrait groups are in the seventeenth-century Dutch tradition, *The Inspectors of the Collegium Medicum of Amsterdam*, 1724, *The Anatomy Lecture of Professor Röell*, 1728, *The Governors of the Orphanage*, 1729, the *Three Governors of the Surgeon's Guild*, 1731, and the *Four Governors of the Institute for the Outdoor Relief of the Poor*, 1740. ¶ *The Anatomy Lecture of Professor Röell*, like the others in the series of 'anatomy lessons,' was painted for the chamber of the Surgeons' Guild in the Weigh House in Amsterdam. Troost's drawing for the composition is similar both in format, with rounded top, and in its arrangements of figures to Rembrandts's *Anatomy Lesson of Dr Deijman* (1656), and it is almost certain that Troost had seen Rembrandt's painting before 1723. Given that Professor Röell was to succeed to Frederick Ruysch in his long praelectorate, and that, at the time Troost received the commission, Röell was already acting *praelector* to Ruysch, it is likely that Troost's painting was destined to hang in the chamber of the Surgeon's Guild in a prominent location, most probably where Rembrandt's picture was placed before it was partially destroyed by the fire of 1723.　¶　It is in fact most probable that Troost was commissioned to paint his Anatomy Lesson in the wake of the severe damage that the fire of 1723 caused to two important anatomy-lesson paintings, the already mentioned Rembrandt's *Dr Deijman*, and an earlier one by Nicolaes Eliasz Pickenoy, *The Anatomy Lesson of Dr Johan Fonteijn* (1625–26). We know, from his preparatory drawing, that Troost's painting was originally intended to be larger than it is now, and that it was meant to include six wardens of the guilds rather than the final three plus an assistant. The reduction in the number of sitters may have been due to the fact that three of the wardens had already been portrayed by Boonen in 1716. Furthermore it appears that Professor Röell, as Ruysch's successor, had not yet given his first lesson in 1728, but was to do so a year later. As Professor Röell was Ruysch's successor, so Troost was Rembrandt's successor in what was the last commission of an Anatomy Lesson by the Amsterdam Surgeons' Guild.[3]　¶　The preparatory drawing shows a fairly grandiose plan, and a composition consistent with other paintings by Troost in its theatrical arrangement, but generic enough when it comes down to the detail of the figure on the dissecting table. This is shown spread out diagonally on the table, with feet in full view and the sole of the left foot fully visible, recalling poses of cadavers in previous paintings, including that in Rembrandt's *Dr Deijman*. The final version of the painting abandons this rather dramatic representation of the corpse for a less confrontational position. In the drawing no dissection has yet taken place, but it is clear, by the way the figure of the *praelector* holds his hand and tools over the corpse's right knee, that this will be the object of the dissection, rather that the more orthodox starting-point of the abdomen, followed by the thorax and head. Two of the three figures of the wardens who remain in the final painting, retain their pose and attire from the drawing. The exception is the figure seated at the back of the dissecting table, who is finally portrayed wearing a hat. He now looks away both from the viewer and from the focus of the scene. His distracted gaze is accompanied by his hand gesture, which is the object of my main observation and hypothesis. His right hand wears a glove. This is not in itself a novel element in sixteenth, seventeenth, and eighteenth century paintings. Gloves, in particular, were of great significance in seventeenth century paintings, continuing a tradition from the Middle Ages when they were associated with cleanliness and authority. By Rembrandt's day they had come to play a symbolic role in a wide variety of ceremonial occasions, from birth and marriage to death, and in everyday rituals of courtesy and etiquette.[4] The custom of holding one or both gloves in a bare hand would appear to be a token of temperate openness and informality. It was a legacy of chivalry, in which the custom of removing one's gauntlet was a sign of peaceful intentions.[5] ¶ The singling out of a gentleman holding or wearing a glove is common in seventeenth and eighteenth century Dutch paintings of anatomy lessons. In Tibout Regters *The Anatomy Lesson of Professor Petrus Camper* (1758), none of the sitters wear hats or gloves except for a man standing at the back of the scene, wearing one glove and holding the other in his bare hand. Another single sitter in Quinkhard's painting of *The Seven Members of the Surgeon's Guild* (1738), holds both gloves in one of his hands. In a later painting by Quinkhard, the *Portrait of the Four Wardens of the Surgeons Guild* (1744), the man who rests his elbow on the chair also holds a glove in his hand. Arnold Boonen's painting of the *Five Wardens of the Surgeon's Guild* (1715–16) also shows only one of the five men holding a glove in his other gloved hand. In an earlier painting of 1670 by Adriaen Backer, *The Anatomy Lesson of Dr Frederick Ruysch*, one of the seven men wears a glove, and holds the other in his left hand. In conclusion, it appears that in group portraits of anatomy lessons only one of the men portrayed wears a glove, and displays one or two, in varying combinations. It is as if only one 'gentleman' stands in for all the other men in the picture, and that they are all, by association, implied and potential owners and wearers of gloves, all honorable as well as cultivated men. ¶ However there is a peculiarity in the glove in Troost's painting which merits a special investigation. This peculiarity is so singular as to suggest that the glove in Troost's painting performs a function which is more specific than general. The sitters in the painting have been identified as Antoni Milan, Bernardus van Vije, and Theodorus van Berckenrode, who wears a glove.[6] Van Berckenrode is seated behind the table where the corpse is stretched out, and rests his right hand on what seems to be a walking stick which has a leather strap, evidently to provide additional support. (FIG) He points with his left hand to the dissected knee, and turns his face and directs his gaze towards the companion who is seated at the side of the table. At this point it is probably worth noting that in other portraits painted by Troost, such as those of a *Gentleman)*, a *Music Lover*, the *Inspectors of the Collegium Medicum in Amsterdam*, *Carel Bouman*, or various portrayals of gentlemen in his numerous genre paintings, he leaves his male figures all with bare hands – there is not a glove in sight. Gloves therefore do not habitually or even routinely feature in Troost's paint-ings. ¶ Theodorus van Berckenrode's glove is not only special for this reason. Surprisingly, it appears to be rather badly worn out. The thumb and the index finger of his hand are exposed, letting the corresponding fingers of the glove hang down. A glove in that condition is unlikely to be a particularly obvious symbol of cleanliness and order, nor could it convey the courtly or dignified status of the man. This glove seems, on the contrary, to signal a necessary function, that of protecting the man's hand from the frequent and vigorous friction exerted by the pressure of his walking stick. Having reached this point, the implication is obvious: Van Berckenrode made regular use of a stick to help him to walk. The problem, we may infer, was in one or both of his legs, or, perhaps, more specifically in one of his knees. It is highly unlikely that the state of health of Theodorus's knee was of such moment to warrant recording in Dutch archives, and it can hardly have been of crucial importance to most viewers of the painting at the time. It may be, therefore, that the specifics of 'his bad knee,' in the context of a painting of a knee dissection, assumes a more generally representative role with respect to clinical anatomy and the surgeon's art. ¶ Troost's realism in portraying the glove extends to the highly praised realism of the corpse, rendered in subtle skin-colours, which range from the pinkish body to the greyish face of the dead man. Troost is thus able to document the effects of hanging on the resulting corpse. The dissection of the knee appears to be accurately rendered: it is performed through the skin, and through the superficial muscle layers. The *praelector* holds open what is probably the knee-joint capsule or *bursa* to expose the muscle and tendons around the patella and possibly the interior of the joint itself. It appears that the visual conventions of the traditional Dutch anatomy lesson, where anatomical demonstrations had a general didactic and philosophical function, are replaced here by a demonstration of clinical anatomy, where the osteo-pathology of the knee is the focus of the dissection. A more restricted philosophical warning, gestured by the gloved man with the knee condition, may intend to remind us that the same could happen to us, 'Know Thy Knee' instead of the more portentous, 'Know Thyself.' Van Berckenrode's own knees are not visible, hidden as they are by the table, but we can deduce that they would be situated roughly in correspondence with those of the stretched-out corpse. The glamorous fashion of the time allows Troost to portray one of the other seated wardens with rather obviously admirable knees clothed in shining fabric. ¶ There also seems to be some significance in allowing one of the sitters to break away from the earlier conventions and the solemnity of Anatomy Lessons. The way that van Berckenrode's gaze is directed at his neighbouring colleague rather than at Professor Röell or the *subjectum*, is a significant departure from earlier conventions of anatomy lessons, such as Rembrandt's *Anatomy of Dr Tulp*, in which the only sitter who turns away from the scene, Adriaen Slabberaen, is not addressing the viewer or his colleagues, but, as William Schupbach points out, looking towards the large volume placed at the feet of the dissected figure.[7] All the other figures in Rembrandt's *Dr Tulp* are absorbed in the event, paying respectful attention to the *praelector* and the actions performed. They all assume what Schupbach describes as 'historical poses' in reinforcing the central narrative.[8]

On the other hand, in Troost's painting there reigns a certain amount of distraction and indifference to the main action, even a certain degree of irony. The audience is clearly identified on our side of the painting, and, as Middelkoop suggests, this may well signal an external audience eager to be educated by the established surgeons. Indeed conventions were changing, and the works commissioned in the eighteenth century by the Surgeons' Guild, as exemplified by Tibout Regters' *Anatomy Lesson of Prof Petrus Camper* of 1758, no longer contained a human corpse, but books and prints, tools, bones or body fragments, and the sitters seemed to be more interested in posing for a portrait, than paying attention to the subject of the scene. ¶ Troost's painting seems to follow a sub-narrative within the main allegory of the elevated status and educative role of the sitters in his Anatomy Lesson. It is a curious and fascinating painting because of its ingenious staging and compellingly rendered details, but it also seems to have greater significance because it stands historically at the end of a period of a hundred years of Amsterdam Surgeons' commissions, in succession to Rembrandt's *Anatomy of Dr Deijman*. As the painting that marks the conclusion of this period, it seems to signal what appears to be a different relationship between the viewer, the sitter, and the subject matter, a new individual and more human message whereby the solemnity of previous Anatomy Lessons is softened by the introduction of a different sort of 'Know Thyself,' a more anecdotal or story-telling reminder of the human condition, by allusion to the specific and common malady of a particular man.

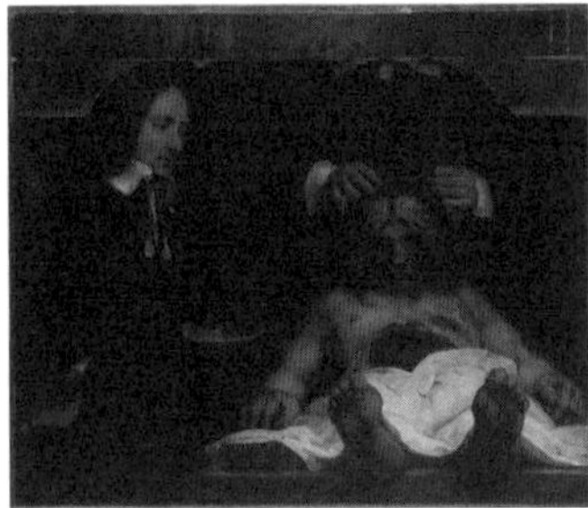

FIGURE 1 Rembrandt van Rijn, *The Anatomy Lesson of Dr Jan Deijman*, 1656, oil on canvas, Amsterdams Historisch Museum.

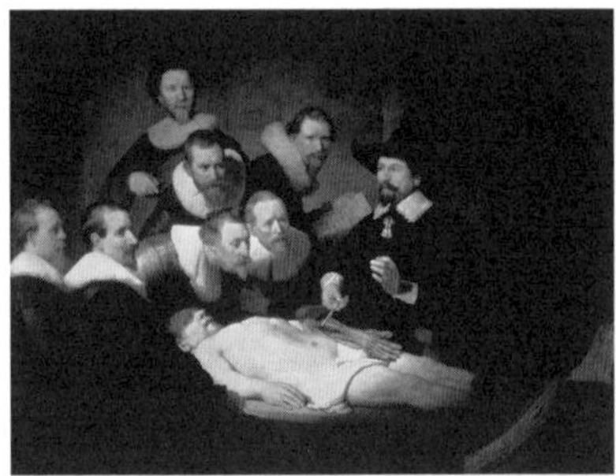

FIGURE 2 Rembrandt van Rijn, *The Anatomy Lesson of Dr Nicolaes Tulp*, 1632, oil on canvas; 169.5 x 216 Mauritshuis, The Hague, The Netherlands/Bridgeman Art Library.

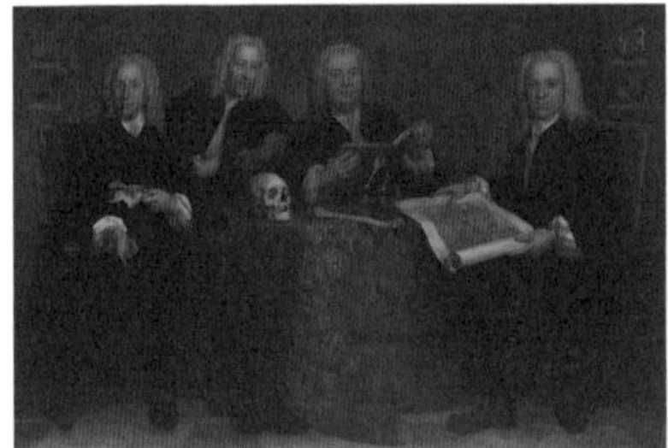

FIGURE 3 Jan Maurits Quinkhard, *Four Wardens of the Surgeons' Guild*, 1744, oil on canvas.

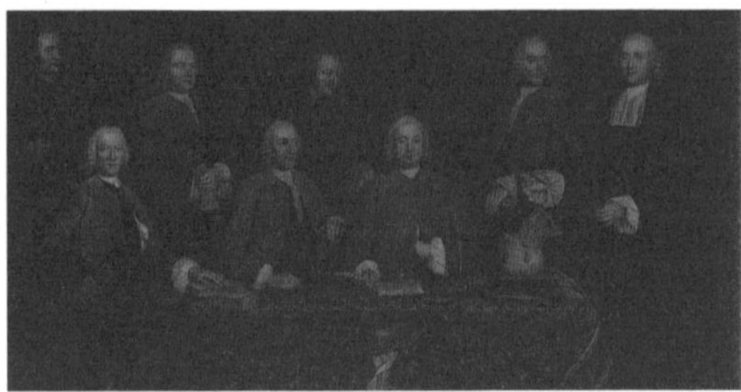

FIGURE 4 Tibout Regters, *The Anatomy Lesson of Professor Petrus Camper*, 1758, oil on canvas, Amsterdams Historisch Museum.

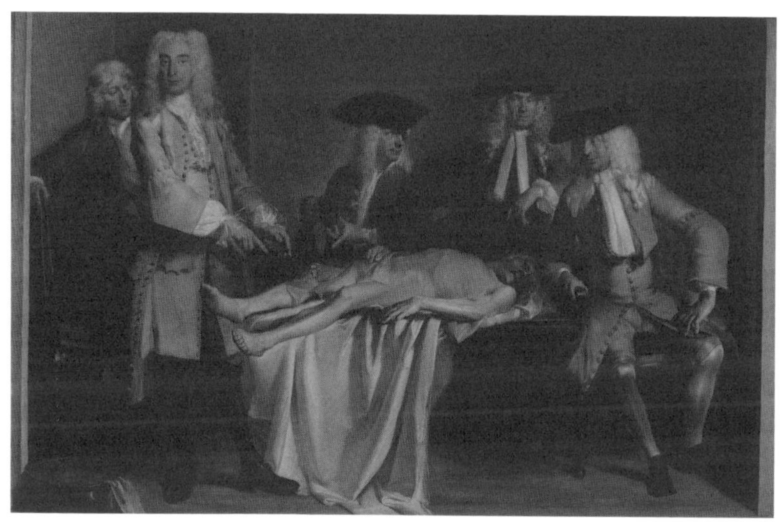

FIGURE 5 and FIGURE 6 (detail) Cornelis Troost, *The Anatomy Lesson of Willem Röell*, 1728, oil on canvas, Amsterdams Historisch Museum.

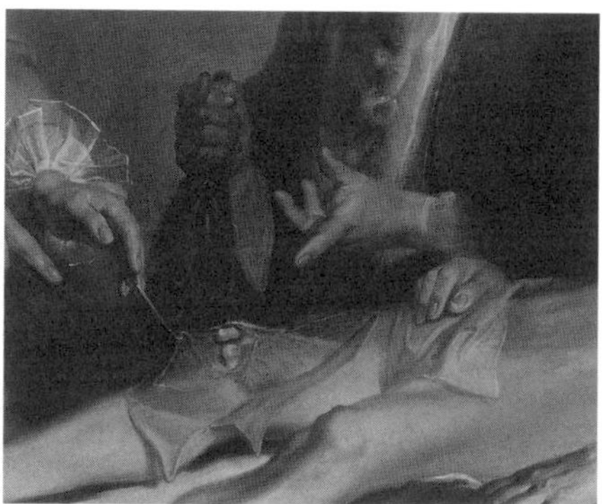

1. J W Niemeijer, *Cornelis Troost, 1696–1750* (Assen: van Gorcum, 1973).

2. See *Cornelis Troost. Painter and Actor*, exhibition catalogue (The Hague: Mauritshuis 1993).

3. Norbert Middelkoop, et all., *Rembrandt Under the Scalpel. The Anatomy Lesson of Dr Nicholaes Tulp dissected* (The Hague: Mauritshuis, 1998–9).

4. David R Smith, 'I Janus: Privacy and the Gentlemanly ideal in Rembrandt's Portrait of Jan Six,' Art History, XI:1 (Mar. 1988): 42–63.

5. *A Cultural History of Gesture: from Antiquity to the Present*, eds., Jan Bremmer and Herman Roodenburg (Cambrdige: Cambridge University Press, 1991).

6. Identified by Niermeijer and signaled by Norbert Middelkoop.

7. William Schupbach, 'The Paradox of Rembrandt's Anatomy of Dr Tulp', London, 1982, in *Medical History, Supplement 2* (London: The Wellcome Trust, 1982).

8. Ibid.

Assimina Kaniari

'Symbolic yet not arbitrary:' perspective as art historical form after Panofsky

Why do we speak of spatially and geometrically conceived structures as expressions of historical content and change in art history today and why do these 'structural-historical' facts imply also culturally contingent entities that describe, at one and the same time, historical and symbolic meaning? Kemp's concept of 'structural intuitions' – a historiographic construct that assumes two culturally distinct lives for two aesthetically similar objects embodied in the form of the structure – has a brief history and one, I would like to argue, that may be seen to be fixed in the contingencies of post-war science, avant-garde art and historians' take to ethnography in the same period.   ¶   The conception of geometry and perspective as 'historical form' – a form that is set to the task of narrating historical change across time and diverse kinds of visual artifacts – has a long history in 20th Century art historical writing. While Panofsky is perhaps the first to have signaled the historiographic potential of perspective, looking at geometrically configured spatial detail as visual evidence for the history of art, perspective as historical form in the historiographic narratives from the late 50s onwards presents significant differences from Panofsky's early concept.[1]   ¶   Not 'philological' detail, but 'ethnographically' extracted detail is the context that all three, Arnheim, Gombrich and finally Martin Kemp, use in their experiments in art historical writing from the post-war period in approaching the idea of perspective as art historical evidence, after Panofsky. Panofsky's widely cited treatment of Dürer's depiction of platonic solids in the engraving of Melancholia I is emblematic of Panofsky's reliance on 'philological' detail to discuss geometrical form as art historical evidence.[2] Dürer's platonic solids comprise, for Panofsky, exemplary sites of iconological-philological description and interpretation while geometrically significant forms acquire in his writings the status of symbolic evidence that point to stories and narratives, such as the Saturnian sense of restriction, tied to the idea of a melancholic temperament seen as symbolically encoded in the motif of the platonic solid. This mediation of symbolic motifs as entities encoded in interpretatively significant narrative, when seen in the act of describing that all three – Arnheim, Gombrich and finally Kemp – perform in their acts of reading geometric form as art historical detail, on the contrary, becomes obsolete. ¶ Art historical content becomes ascribed to the idea of geometric form via an irreducibly 'ethnographic' sensibility. It is no longer a question of meaning and content being fixed in the philological testimony of sources past which transcribes geometrical detail into art historical explanation, but contingencies that originate from the present and the peculiar circumstances of Arnheim, Gombrich and Kemp's own cultural context. This gives rise to the key framework of reference in the context of analogy. Post-war science and avant-garde art, in particular, may be seen to comprise two of the contexts three authors privilege in their experiments with ethnographic analogy and art historical description. ¶ The parallel universe of both scientists' and avant garde artists' practices forms the site of analogy for all three (Arnheim, Gombrich and Kemp). In thinking about geometric form as art historical evidence in an ethnographic light and in the context of modern science and avant-garde art, Arnheim, Gombrich and Kemp reference but also revisit Panofsky's early concept of perspective as historical form.

'Symbolic yet not arbitrary'

Kemp's important distinction and advocacy of a 'symbolic' yet 'not arbitrary' reading of perspective illustrates most clearly this switch from an earlier methodological apparatus to the new one encountered in post-war art history and one that is much active still today.[3] Perspective for Kemp expresses a cultural entity but also a material and physical thing. It is Kemp's 'materialism' that allows for this definition of perspective as symbolic, yet not arbitrary form, in turn. Real and physical parameters concerned with the creation of the work, its material properties and the ways of seeing and doing that artists and scientists engage with in given historical and social contexts, participate as contexts active in Kemp's conception of perspective as 'symbolic yet not arbitrary' form. ¶ By contrast to Panofsky's conceptual appropriation of geometric form into symbolic motif that may be decoded in art history via philological research, narrative and obsessively 'textual' scrutiny, post-war treatments of perspective turn to concepts drawn from modern science in rethinking the question of geometrically defined form as art historical evidence. Both Arnheim and Gombrich appropriate modern science in their revisionist writing. Kemp's historiography nevertheless departs in many ways from both Arnheim and Gombrich's experiments in art historical writing with modern science. ¶ On the one hand, all three authors share a vocabulary that may be traced back to the introduction of gestalt theory in art historical writing on perspective, evident in discussions about geometrically configured form in art as an expression of visual 'order.'[4] By contrast to the concept of 'visual order' that emerges in the writings of Arnheim and Gombrich, being in direct analogy to gestalt theory and the psychology of vision, order for Kemp is a matter pertinent to the domain of theoretical biology. Kemp draws on biological concepts and theories that emerge in the post-war period.[5] D'Arcy Thompson's writings, hugely influential among modernist and avant-garde art circles from the late 40s onwards and among contemporary architects interested in complexity mediate, I would like to argue, Martin Kemp's concept of geometric form as historical evidence in his history of the visual and treatment of perspective and geometry as art historical form.[6]

Kemp's ethnographic eye and Thompson's 'materialism'

Thompson's definition of form is a model which Kemp uses to discuss geometric syntax in art and mediates Kemp's analysis of geometric order as art historical form. Kemp's 'subtle materialism' may be seen as an implication of this appropriation, conceptual and methodological. In looking at Goldsworthy's work and solution to the problem of form, Kemp, for example, gives priority to physical and material considerations connected to the creation of the work. Visual order for Kemp is a question contingent on both cultural and material reality; it is symbolic, in terms of cultural content yet real, in a physical sense, object. The understanding of form and geometric order as the effect of physical parameters is in place in 1917 in biological analysis of developmental phenomena in the writings of D'Arcy Thompson and his book *On Growth and Form*.[7] Privileging the idea of 'physical considerations' in the explanation of geometrical detail in natural as well as artificial form,[8] Thompson asserted in the second edition of the book in 1942: 'We want to see how in some cases at least, the forms of living things, and of the parts of living things, can be explained by physical considerations.'[9] ¶ In his treatment of Goldsworthy's form and geometric solution to the problem of form, Kemp references the same notion: 'Through site, touch and motion he searches out morphological commonalities which arise from the material and processes of nature,'[10] Kemp writes on account of Goldsworthy's work. Herbert Read's writings on abstraction and proportion, as well as Moholy-Nagy's axioms for modern design, prior to Kemp's writings, attempted to establish the same dialogue between this biological text and conception of form and revisionist writing on art.[11] Nagy's discussion of the 'linear mobility' knot-like image from *Vision in Motion*, for example, is an attempt to articulate on a theoretical-revisionist ground 'axioms' for modern design. This references Thompson's notion of form as the site where 'forces act upon matter.' ¶ Nagy explicitly acknowledges the connection between Thompson's concept of form and his own. 'I find an almost identical statement in the book "Form in Growth," by Sir D'Arcy Wentworth Thompson (Cambridge University Press, 1942), p.16,' he writes, citing the relevant text where Thompson defines 'the form of an object as a diagram of forces.'[12] Furthermore, Nagy's discussion of axioms comprises a number of examples that reference the impact of natural forces on styles of pattern in nature as the result of material considerations. 'The sea rolls against a sandy beach: the waves subtly corrugate the sand. A painted wall cracks; the surface becomes a web of fine lines ... Rope falls; it lies in smooth curves on the ground.'[13] "All these phenomena, caused by various processes,' Nagy concludes, 'can be understood as diagrams in space representing forces acting upon the varied materials plus the resistance of the materials to the impact of these forces.'[14]

This conception of natural pattern, as the effect of forces that act upon matter in nature, re-emerges in the words that Goldsworthy uses to describe his own work and which Kemp's cites in his analysis of Goldsworthy's solution to the problem of form as a geometrically specific solution.   ¶   The comparison between natural and artificial form is mediated by the idea of natural pattern in Goldsworthy's thought process, Kemp insists in citing the artist's words: 'Works that have the qualities of snaking but are not snakes.'[15] The writings of post-war scientists, such as Waddington himself, may be seen, in turn, to have triggered Kemp's interest in Thompson as a site for art historical analogy, in the first place.   ¶   In *Seen-Unseen* Kemp explicitly acknowledges the impact of C H Waddington's writings on his own concept of structural intuitions. 'My approach exhibits some affinities with Conrad Hal Waddington's *Behind Appearance* published in 1969,' Kemp writes linking the concept of structural intuitions to Thompson via Waddington and continues:[16]

Waddington, Professor of Animal Genetics in Edinburgh was married to the architect Margaret Justin Blanco White, and enjoyed contact with a number of leading artists from the 1930s onwards, including John and Mary Myfanwy Piper, Henry Moore, Ben Nicholson, Barbara Hepworth, Ivon Hitchens, Alexander Calder, Lázló Moholy-Nagy, and Walter Gropius. He illustrates a series of important works by Modernist artists, with a strong emphasis on abstraction from nature, together with images from twentieth-century science that appear to betray similar organizational principles. His suggestive mingling of art and science begins to do the kind of visual job with which I am concerned, but lacks a developed explanatory framework – whether historical or theoretical. The three areas I will be considering in my own attempt to illuminate 'structural intuitions' can be labeled, somewhat crudely, as 'structure,' the 'splash,' and 'the geometry of growth.'[17]

In the mid 60s 'structurally' conceived comparisons between art and science are in place in a number of writings by scientists, art historians but also of philosophers and historians of science who like Thomas Kuhn explored the potential of ethnographic method for historiographic revision. Kuhn's writings from the late 60s give us a glimpse of the tensions and controversies inherent in the post-war ethnographic turn of historical thinking concerned with art, science and the social and the dialogue between the three as the novel focus for 'interdisciplinary' research. ¶ The question of art's 'relation' to science for Kuhn emerges as a question and a problem that while historically specific may be explored adequately only in the context of sociological analysis. Kuhn's ethnographies of art and science are not only concerned with the communities and practices of artists and scientists only but also with those of art historians, as Kuhn's frequent references to Panofsky and Gombrich show. This is also true of his dialogue with George Kubler and James Ackerman.[18] ¶ Kuhn's writings are mediated by historiographic constructs derived from the writings of art historians, such as Panofsky's on perspective and Gombrich's on order, but also give rise to the creation of further discourse and controversy in the context of art history; Ackerman attempts to extend Kuhn's concepts in art historical explanation and historiography while Kubler attacks Kuhn's analysis of art and science relations as 'ethological' remarks. According to Kubler, it was the present of art and art's unique visual characteristics following its engagement with science and technology that become obsolete in Kuhn's theorizing.[19] Referring to this engagement as the 'new reality' in art and science, Kubler isolates the visual and social characteristics emergent in this form of art which for him coincides with avant-garde art itself.

New reality, structures and avant-garde experiments in art and science
Already from the early 50s, Kubler's 'new reality' is visible in the writings and experiments of artists with modern science and technology. In this context, increasing numbers of artists develop a particular interest in the idea of pattern and structure as the privileged site where comparisons between art and science become apparent. These are not so much about artists' and scientists' epistemologically equivalent jobs but on the contrary about connections between art and science at the level of the social. It is to these experiments, aesthetic, material, visual and social that post war scientists and art historians discussing art and science relations turn to as the site of ethnographic analogy for the discussion of

art as a whole. ¶ Waddington's parallels between nature and artifice as comparisons between styles of visual order embodied in natural and artificial pattern are mediated, for example, by examples of modernist and avant-garde art form contemporary to Waddington's own context.[20] If abstraction art is of particular interest to Waddington for his analogies, a number of works from the 1950s onwards embrace an irreducibly abstracted imagery that is seen as the result of new imaging techniques applied on art. New imaging techniques not only construct new aesthetics, in the form of avant-garde art practices, but they are also thought to lead to a new understanding of biological phenomena via a new kind of visibility. The re-discovery of Thompson's book by post-war avant-garde artists and of its profusely illustrated explanations of phenomena previously inaccessible to the naked eye including abstracted and structural expressions of micro-visions of nature and art that attested to an uncanny behaviour of matter at this scale, is a phenomenon not least concerned with this contingency, historical and social.[21] ¶ The 1951 ICA show *On Growth and Form* confirms this post-war revival of interest in Thompson in the arts and the avant-garde arts in particular referencing directly visual and conceptual registers encountered in Thompson's definition and visualization of form. This revival is frequently matched by post-war scientists' own discourse together with the writings of art theorists and critics and historians, as the programme of the symposium of the ICA exhibition demonstrates. As Lancelot Law Whyte writes in 1951 in the proceedings of the symposium, *Aspects of Form*, Thompson's theoretical and 'biological' definition of form presented artists, scientists and art critics with unique opportunities for the creation of an interdisciplinary dialogue between art and science.[22] ¶ The symposium and the 1951 ICA show were both part of the Festival of Britain 1951 concerned with the merging of industry and science in the post-war period one century after The Great Exhibition of 1851. Modern design and industrial design occupied a leading role in the Festival and on many occasions connections were forged between structures derived from novel scientific and technological advances applied to the observation of the natural world and the principles of modern design applied to artifice as well as art. While Thompson had defined form as an irreducibly dynamic entity, in the book that accompanied the symposium, edited by Whyte, authors such as C H Waddington, Rudolph Arnheim, Herbert Read and Ernst Gombrich argued for the importance of form, understood as an irreducibly dynamic and structural entity, to the emergence of an interdisciplinary dialogue between art and science.[23] (FIG 2 and 3) Thompson defined 'form' as the site where phenomena of 'growth' had emerged. Arnheim, on the other hand, discussed form in art as the expression of the idea of process while Whyte referred to the idea of 'states of order,' a concept which re-merged in Arnheim's other work as an analogy to the idea of entropy and via a reference to Whyte himself.[24] It was a number of 'elementary' forms that had occupied Thompson's attention to in his book however, in particular, and in this light, the geometric forms of 'platonic solids' depicted by Dürer in his engraving of Melancholia I and earlier Leonardo in his illustrations of Pacioli's *De Divina Proporzione* were also part of the book, this time, via Haeckel's illustration of radiolarians based on Haeckel's alleged observations under the microscope[25] (FIG 1). Most importantly, it was the same attention to elementary forms as expressions of intransient aspects, this time, of a social reality, and the reality of modern life, in particular that comprised the focus of the 1951 ICA exhibition curated by Richard Hamilton, as well as of a later show, curated at the same venue by Paolozzi, Henderson and the Smithsons. ¶ *The Parallels of Life and Art* 1953 ICA show, as in the 1951 exhibition which referenced the idea of structure as a site of analogy between art and science establishing thus visual 'parallels' between 'life and art'. 'Technical inventions such as the photographic enlarger, aerial photography, and the high speed flash have given us new tools, with which to expand our field of vision beyond the limits imposed on previous generations,' the 'editors' of the show declared, adding that, newspapers, periodicals and film had made such imagery widely available.[26] 'Their products feed our newspapers, our periodicals and our films' and they are 'continually before our eyes,' a Memorandum of the show kept at Tate Archive asserted, concluding that 'material' and 'aspects of material' 'hitherto inaccessible' could now become witnessed given the new enhanced landscape of communication and visibility.[27] Like Nagy's structures linking reality with art practice, accessibility, in the context of art discussed in the memo, concerned the 'visual world' which lay 'beneath the microscope,' and not the 'ordinary world.' The former is a source of inspiration which could 'excite' the painter's senses.[28] Structures, as Nigel Henderson and the 'editors' of the show asserted in the *Parallels of Life and Art* memo, allowed one's visual access to segments of reality previously inaccessible via one's transfer across scales and from the micro to the macro, at the visual level. ¶ Aesthetic similarity among images drawn from both life and art, if accessed at that 'structural' and abstract level, expressed, the 'editors' argued, evidence of cultural cohesion between life, industry and art. Elementary forms and their images, captured against a number of modern technological devices, not only expressed examples of visually abstracted aspects of material reality that were previously inaccessible and against normal scales of vision. Yet, in isolating intransient expressions of reality from the constant and macroscopic view of flux that characterized the experience of modern life, states of order detectable in the visual level and concerned with society rather than nature were also revealed. Kemp's notion of perspective as 'symbolic, yet not arbitrary' form may be seen to contain this tension in post-war historical thinking concerned with the attempt to integrate ethnographic and sociological practice in historical analysis by taking into consideration the contingencies of post-war art and science, as its key sites of ethnographic practice. ¶ According to Kemp, structures as abstracted and elementary visual geometrical forms are not evidence of inherent 'natural' connections between art and science. On the contrary, they stand as evidence for the cultural cohesion between art, science and society in the modern world and modern art history that follows but also revisits the writings of Erwin Panofsky.

Ethnographic practice and 'subtle materialism' in Kemp's writing
While 'symbolic,' Kemp's geometrical forms-art historical evidence are not 'arbitrary' in the sense that a semiotic reading of visual detail and syntax would require. Material properties and Kemp's subtle materialism allow for the synthesis between

these two seemingly conflicting notions: the symbolic and the non arbitrary in his reading of perspective and revisiting of Panofsky's early concept.[29] Kemp's structural intuitions, in this light, are an extraordinary act of synthesis that has attempted and succeeded in reformulating a long tradition of writing against the material and historical contingencies of the work under study. In this sense, they also are a historiographic act, as well.[30] As Loisidi has noted, structures have longed grasped the imaginary of artists and art historians often posing insolvable questions for the art historian who attempts to provide a historically justified explanation of particular structures connected to particular historical and social contexts that re-emerge in periods where no chronologically or sociologically conceived causal links could be forged.[31] This presence – and also resistance – of structures to the act of art historical explanation transcribes revision into an essentially creative act; one that has to reconsider the relation between tangible reality, its physical structure, with the pre-existing art historical analytical apparatus and the contingencies of social and historical context of a given moment.   ¶   Kemp's 'structural intuitions' as a revisionist-creative act builds and reformulates the pre-existing tradition of writing about perspective and geometric form as historical objects that emerges in 20th century writing.[32] Kemp's concept of perspective as art historical form, while embodied via Kemp's ethnographic eye in the traditions of seeing of post-war art and science, builds clearly on a number of predecessors, Arnheim being one of them.   ¶   The very term and concept of 'visual order' is one in which Arnheim was particularly interested in, as expression, not of subjective and psychologically conceived 'intention' on behalf of the artist, but as the embodiment and expression of a thresholds fixed and contingent on material properties and physical laws as well as aesthetic and structurally conveyed 'detail.' As Daskalothanasis's reading of De Chirico's 'perspective' shows, Arnheim's concept of visual order at times 'tinted' and clashed with the artists' own conception of geometrical form, De Chirico's geometric syntax in his metaphysical painting being one such example. According to Daskalothanasis, the order of De Chirico's metaphysical space may hardly be seen to express the notion of a visually and spatially coherent and uniform space that Arnheim's use of the term visual order projected on De Chirico's perspective implies.[33] Arnheim's reading of De Chirico's perspective, being prototypical, thus, constructs, as much as describes De Chirico's perspective and concept of perspective, transmuting the artist's metaphysical ambiguity into an expression of visual order in the post-war gestalt sense privileged by Arnheim in his analysis of geometric syntax. ¶ This is not a point about historical accuracy. Rather it testifies to the changing nature of art historical practice and inference that concepts of perspective manifest between Arnheim's perspective and Kemp's 'symbolic yet not arbitrary' geometric form. If philological detail was essential to Panofsky, seeing in art history for Arnheim is almost a neutral extension of a physiological vision.[34] ¶ One of the outstanding feats that may be credited to Martin Kemp's work deals precisely with the synthesis of these two opposing threads in the methodology of art history. Panofsky's and Arnheim's forms, following Martin Kemp's synthesis, are no longer two parallel and disconnected entities in the long historiography of art. Kemp's 'new history of the visual' and 'structural intuitions' express creative-historiographic constructs that bridge these two seemingly contrasting analytical styles and traditions. In doing so, structural intuitions become historical objects important in their own right. On the one hand, Kemp's writing has always expressed a fascination for transitions in thought styles across the medieval and renaissance divide. Nevertheless, Kemp's style of thinking and seeing, as far as his art historical writing is concerned, is above all the result of social and material contingencies associated with the rise to Modernism. It is grounded, in particular, in the post-war period that gave rise to social-visual and material experiments in avant-garde art and science. In this paper, I have tried to grasp the connection between the art historian and the style of art historical writing as one of analogy, a concept very dear to Kemp, who once described himself to me as a medieval man. ¶ To discern the modernist art historian in the medieval man has been an act of seeing rich in historiographic detail and historical consequence, but above all, an act of recognizing methodological revision across the broad range of 20th century art historical writing. Martin Kemp's concept of perspective as 'symbolic yet not arbitrary' form and the novel take on

art historical materialism that the latter implies and entails merits significant consideration, if one wishes to map and assess this territory.

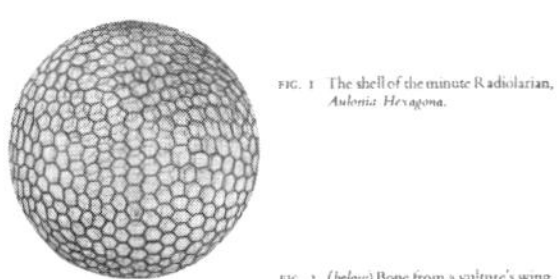

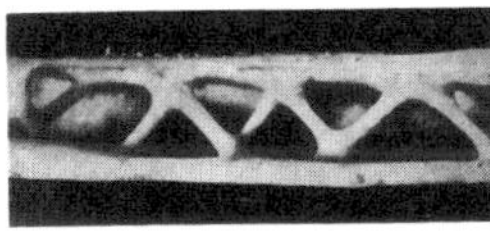

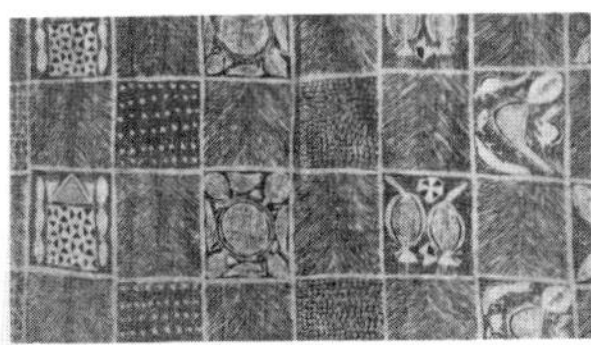

FIGURE 2 'The shell of the minute Radiolarian,' 'Bone from a vulture's wing to show internal structure,' 'Native dyed textile from Nigeria.' Comparisons of natural to artificial structure from Waddington, 'The character of biological form,' in Whyte (ed.), *Aspects of Form*, 1951, p.53.

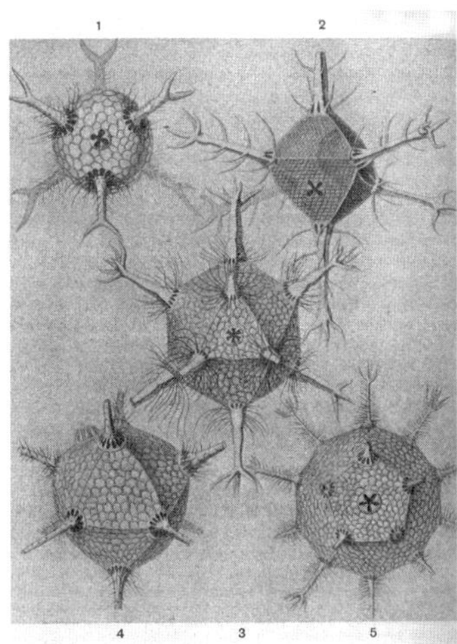

FIGURE 1 Skeletons of various Radiolarians, after Haeckel.' Illustration of radiolarians from Thompson, *On Growth and Form*, 1942, p.726.

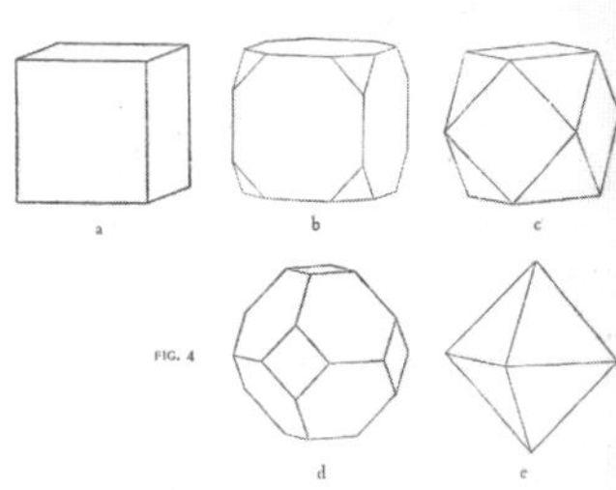

FIGURE 3 'Types of face which a real crystal shows as dependent by the relative rates of growth of the types,' from Humphreys-Owen, 'Physical Principles underlying inorganic form', in Whyte (ed.), *Aspects of Form*, 1951, p.17.

With thanks to Sara Thornton.

1. E Panofsky, 'Die Perspektive als Symbolische Form,' in *Vorträge der Bibliothek Warburg*, 1924–25, Leipzig, Berlin, 1927, pp.258–330.

2. As Yates notes, the interpretation of this engraving as a representation of inspired melancholy was first put forward in a study in German by Panofsky and Saxl published in 1923, it was again discussed by Panofsky in his book on Dürer published in 1945 and was fully expounded in the work *Saturn and Melancholy* by Klibansky, Panofsky, and Saxl published in 1964. See F. Yates, 'Chapman and Dürer on Inspired Melancholy,' *University of Rochester Library Bulletin* 34 (1981). http://www.lib.rochester.edu/index.cfm?PAGE=3566b.

3. M Kemp, *Seen | Unseen: Art, science and Intuition from Leonardo to the Hubble Telescope*, Oxford, 2006. See also my review of the book in *Science Studies* for a presentation of this concept as a materialist rather than realist position. A Kaniari, Book review of Martin Kemp's *Seen | Unseen: Art, science and Intuition from Leonardo to the Hubble Telescope*, Oxford, 2006, *Science Studies. An interdisciplinary journal for science and technology studies*, 22, 1 (2008) pp.83–85.

4. For the articulation of this notion as a boundary between earlier writing and thinking on proportion and the post-war tradition see Herbert Read's discussion of self-organization and perception in H Read, 'Preface,' in *Aspects of Form*, L L Whyte (ed.), London, 1951, pp.v–vi, p.v.

5. Gombrich's discussion of the duck-rabbit image is exemplary of his interest in gestalt. Wittgenstein earlier had devoted a considerable amount of discussion to this image while Gombrich at the end of his *Art and Illusion* will only be too keen to acknowledge this connection by explicitly referencing *Philosophical Investigations* reproducing however an image not from Wittgenstein, but from a publication on gestalt psychology instead. See E. H. Gombrich, *Art and Illusion: A study in the psychology of pictorial representation*, New York, 1960, p.335, 361. See also R Arnheim, *Visual Thinking*, California, 1969.

6. In *Seen | Unseen* Kemp discusses Thompson both in the context of modern science as well as modern art. The legacy of D'Arcy Thompson's 'geometry of growth' on contemporary scientific practice comprises one of the book's chapters. See Kemp, *Seen | Unseen*.

7. D'Arcy Thompson's theoretical definition of form appears in his book *On Growth and Form* first published in 1917 and re-appearing as second revised edition in 1942.

8. D'Arcy Thompson, *On Growth and Form*, Cambridge, 1942, p.15.

9. Ibid.

10. M Kemp, *Seen | Unseen*, p.215.

11. See L Maholy-Nagy, *Vision in Motion*, Chicago, 1947 and H Read, *Design and Industry*, London, 1934.

12. Maholy-Nagy, *Vision in Motion*, p.36.

13. Maholy-Nagy, *Vision in Motion*, p.36.

14. Maholy-Nagy, *Vision in Motion*, p.36.

15. Kemp, *Seen | Unseen*, p.215.

16. Kemp, *Seen | Unseen*, p.211.

17. Ibid.

18. T S Kuhn, 'The History of Science,' *The Essential Tension. Selected Studies in Scientific Tradition and Change*, Chicago, 1977, pp.105-126, p.125; T S Kuhn, 'The relations between history and the history of science,'*The Essential Tension. Selected Studies in Scientific Tradition and Change*, Chicago, 1977, pp.127–164, p.153.

19. See T Kuhn, '[The new reality in art and science] Comment,' *Comparative Studies in Society and History. Special Issue on Cultural Innovation* 11, 4 (Oct. 1969), pp.403–412, p.407. Kuhn's 'Comment', later

reproduced in the *Essential Tension* was first published in 1969, the special edition of *Comparative Studies in Society and History* devoted to 'Cultural Innovation' included as contributors George Kubler, consulting editor for the quarterly and Art Historian at Yale University, James Ackerman, E M Hafner, S N Eisenstadt and Thomas S Kuhn. The papers, as Raymond Grew confirmed in the Introduction, were first presented at a three-day conference in Ann Arbor in May 1967. Art in the context of the conference discussed avant-garde art and the 'new reality' in art and science in particular. See also the papers by J Ackerman, 'The demise of the avant-garde: notes of the sociology of recent American art,' *Comparative Studies in Society and History*, 11, 4 (Oct. 1969), pp.371–384, p.371 and G Kubler, '[The new reality in art and science]: Comment,' *Comparative Studies in Society and History* 11, 4 (Oct. 1969), pp.398–402, p.402 in the same volume.

20. See C H Waddington, *Behind Appearance: a study of the relations between painting and the natural sciences in this century*, Edinburgh, 1969.

21. See however on the other hand Thompson's reliance on 19th century authors such as Haeckel as well as a 'platonic' sense of order employed in discussing form and structure in nature in the 20th century that transcend the necessity of technology to visualize intransient form. Thompson, on the other hand, makes himself the claim that the book is about mathematics linking Plato and platonic solids to Haeckel, the microscope and the Pythagorians.

22. *Aspects of Form: a symposium on form in nature and art*, L L Whyte (ed.), London, 1951.

23. See E H Gombrich, 'Meditations on a hobby hose, or the roots of artistic form,' in *Aspects of Form: a symposium on form in nature and art*, L L Whyte (ed.), London, 1951, pp.209–228; C H Waddington, 'The character of biological form,' in *Aspects of Form: a symposium on form in nature and art*, L L Whyte (ed.), London, 1951, pp.43–56; R Arnheim, 'Gestalt Psychology and artistic form,' in *Aspects of Form: a symposium on form in nature and art*, L L Whyte (ed.), London, 1951, pp.196–208.

24. R Arnheim, *Entropy and art: an essay on disorder and order*, Berkeley, 1971.

25. Thompson, *On Growth and Form*, p.726.

26. Tate archive, Henderson Papers, 9211–5–1–1.

27. Tate archive, Henderson Papers, 9211–5–1–1.

28. Tate archive, Henderson Papers, 9211–5–1–1.

29. It's worth emphasizing here also the Kantian context, via Cassirer, for Panofsky's perspective as symbolic form. Even though Martin Kemp's 'structural intuitions' might sound Kantian, according to Kemp himself, "the tightly knit interplay of structures in nature and cognitive structures does not involve Kantian imposition of a priori mental structures on nature to create space, time etc.," hence the association is not pursued here any further as a link between Panofsky's and Kemp's concepts of perspective as historical forms. Martin Kemp, Pers. com. On the contrary, Martin Kemp adds to Panofsky's 3 types of symbolic communication another which involves a kind of "'real metaphor," as he calls it. Martin Kemp, Pers. Com. An example that he kindly offered in relation to this notion and for the purpose of this paper would be "a lion to denote a brave or fierce person". Kemp, Pers. Com. "The symbol is non-arbitrary because it relies upon aspects of a lion's behaviour, and can be understood quire readily by a wide range of viewers (without knowing the mediaeval bestiary, for instance)," Kemp asserts, noting that, "I suppose that is a kind of 'structure' as well, and is ubiquitous in allegory (corresponding to Dante's 2nd level of interpretation." Many thanks to Martin Kemp for all comments and responses to my paper.

30. Many thanks to N Loisidi for the idea of historiography as a creative act.

31. Niki Loisidi, Pers. Com.

32. Kemp is also aware of other forms of thinking in a scientific light that are not structurally or visually embedded and has considered their ability, absence or failure to explain art in art historical discourse against his prevalent 'structural intuitions.' In one of his e-mails to me commenting on the essay he

draws this distinction. 'One further thought. I am not claiming that all art of
science works with structural intuitions. There are clearly other modes of thought in science
– *eg* algebraic, which is non-visual. I wasn't intending it to cover all visual arts, but maybe it does to
some degree. Needs thinking about.' Martin Kemp, Pers. Com.

33. N Daskalothanasis, *The painting of Giorgio De Chirico: the syntax of metaphysical space*, Athens, 2001;
    *Ν Δασκαλοθανάσης, Η ζωγραφική του Giorgio De Chirico: Η σύνταξη του μεταφυσικού
    χώρου, Αθήνα,* 2001. Many thanks to N. Daskalothanasis for reading and commenting on an early
    draft of my essay.

34. I copy here Martin Kemp's response to my paper and to my making of his writing into an act of
    'thick description', that is an ethnographically specific practice. 'Assimina, This is very generous
    – and makes me think! It is interesting to be aligned with ethnography, when I have never
    really actively engaged with it. Odd how I got there! The excerpt I sent of the Portguese essay
    picks up on the way that enduring structures appear (and sometimes cannot appear) in historical
    terms. I never met Arnheim, but corresponded with him. We shared a lot in common. I did not
    subscribe to Gestalt theory as such, but its underlying drift seemed productive. E H G greatly
    respected Arnheim. I love the Nagy material – not known to me!' Martin Kemp, Pers. Com.

Claire Farago

Redemptive acts of seeing: Riegl's Australian legacy

For Martin

Contemporary inquiries into the structural intuitions shared by artists and scientists, a subject of enduring interest to Martin Kemp, are directly implicated in the movement of ideas that is the subject of the present essay. It is offered as a thought experiment, a mental exercise somewhat in the manner of Leonardo da Vinci's Scholastic mode of investigating a problem by imagining an experiment. Occasionally, it is difficult to tell from Leonardo's notebooks whether we are dealing with the documentation of a thought experiment or of an actual laboratory procedure. There is a similar indeterminacy in what follows here between the entirely hypothetical and the merely analogous: I ask the reader to imagine whether and how European structures of seeing and theories of perception, in particular those explored by art historian Aloïs Riegl (1858–1905) around the turn of the twentieth century, found their way into the institutional perception of contemporary Australian Aboriginal painting. ¶ By the end of the eighteenth century, an international discourse of European origin had been established for representing indigenous peoples as examples of primordial humans, with Australian Aboriginals as the most primitive of all.[1] Then towards the end of the nineteenth century, E B Tylor's (1832–1917) *Primitive Culture* (1871) set the stage for new definitions of art as a universal phenomenon. He suggested that all areas of culture can be comprehended as one natural process rooted in primitive savagery. With this move, cultural differences came to be explained in terms of degrees of cultural progress through which every society passes. In 1885, Tylor recruited his student Baldwin Spencer (1860–1929) to relocate the Pitt Rivers collection of ethnographic artifacts to Oxford, where this account of shared cultural evolution was famously displayed in a museum setting.[2] Two years later, Bachelor's degree in hand, Spencer emigrated to Australia to take up a position in biology at the University of Melbourne, where he was appointed honorary director of the Museum of Victoria in 1899. Over his long productive career, Spencer assembled an unprecedented collection of artifacts, photographs, and the earliest films on Aboriginal peoples based on his own fieldwork.[3]   ¶   Baldwin Spencer's first book, *Native Tribes of Central Australia* (1899), and two subsequent volumes, widely considered as groundbreaking studies, had an important influence on European theories of societal development. On the one hand, as David Tacey writes, Spencer's writings document the envy and spiritual longing of Europeans looking at indigenous cosmology of place and spiritual mythology.[4] On the other hand, following ideas popular at the time, Spencer's widely disseminated publications problematically cast contemporary indigenous Australians as primitives playing the role of Europe's past.[5] Emile Durkheim's (1858–1917) *Elementary Forms of Religion* (1912) relied heavily on the published work of Spencer and his collaborator Frank Gillen (1855–1912), as did Sigmund Freud's *Totem and Taboo: Some Points of Agreement between the Mental Lives of Savages and Neurotics* (1913). Yet there is a third component of Spencer's legacy to consider: the high cultural value that he and a few of his contemporaries attributed to Aboriginal cultural artifacts.[6] The field notes and specimens of Spencer's collecting activities include an irreplaceable archive of ethnographic photographs and films recording indigenous Australian ceremonies and daily activities. The organization of the material collected (his descriptions, classificatory schemes, and so on) encapsulates in its structure the system of his beliefs about Aboriginal society, which merits study in its own right. At the same time, this material record is available today, archived at Melbourne's foremost educational and museological institutions, to construct new ways of looking at the past.   ¶   The following story of Riegl's hypothetical Australian legacy is haunted by these broader historical circumstances. I would like to begin by suggesting that a previously unrecognized translation of Riegl's ideas to Australia can be traced through the activities of a lone art teacher named Geoffrey Bardon (1940–2003) working with indigenous artists of the central Western Desert in 1971–72 (FIG 1). Bardon introduced acrylic paint and canvas to a group of senior Aboriginal men living in the government settlement of Papunya, located 250 kilometres northwest of Alice Springs in the central Western desert region of the Northern Territory. In the late 1980s, the art movement that had begun as an educational program at Papunya achieved world-wide recognition that brought new respect for Aboriginal peoples throughout Australia and the world.[7] Of course, a complete account of the historical, political, and social factors that enabled the emergence of contemporary Aboriginal painting is far more complex, as Philip Batty, Senior Curator of Indigenous Cultures at the Museum Victoria today, writes:

> *Aboriginal men such as Kaapa Tjampitjinpa and others had been depicting ceremonial iconography in acrylic and watercolor paintings long before Bardon arrived at Papunya. As Bardon himself indicated, the 'big break' that sparked the out-pouring of 'Papunya Boards' in 1971–72 occurred when Kaapa won the lucrative 'Caltex Prize' in 1971. The winning painting was not entered by Bardon, but by a local government officer, Jack Cook – the kind of person that Bardon presumably despised. Bardon reported that when Kaapa returned to Papunya with the prize money, there was a clamor for art materials from a number of men (I knew Kaapa well – a very mercurial character who would have delighted in boasting about his win!) Moreover, the so-called 'Renaissance' of Aboriginal art at Papunya was in actuality the product of a long engagement/exchange between Aboriginals and Whites in Central Australia stretching back to at least the 1920s. This is not to say that Bardon did not play a significant role – he did. Most importantly, he established a precedent and model for 'white art advisors' who have been indispensable in the development of the Aboriginal art industry (and I don't mean that in a negative sense).[8]*

Philip Batty and Judith Ryan, Curator of Aboriginal Art at the National Gallery of Victoria in Melbourne, are currently preparing a major exhibition on the formative period of the Western Desert Art Movement.[9] My concern in the present essay is with what Michel Foucault has called the processes of recuperation, the recasting of prior representations in new form.[10] When we search for the invisible coordinates of race, writes Ann Stoler in her brilliant application of Foucault's analysis of state racism to the extra-European colonial world, the linkages between visual and verbal forms of knowledge should be stressed.[11] The same applies to the present case. Specifically, I am trying to understand what role was played by European accounts of structures of seeing in the emergence and later success of contemporary Aboriginal painting.   ¶   It is unlikely that Bardon knew Riegl's work directly and, in fact, he may never have even heard of the Viennese art historian. Yet Bardon knew and utilized Riegl's famous distinction between two different modes of perception modeled on the senses of sight and touch. Their likely intermediary was the Austrian-born American art educator Viktor Lowenfeld (1903–1960), author of arguably the most influential textbook in art education during the latter half of the twentieth century.[12] Lowenfeld initially studied art at the University of Vienna about twenty years after Riegl himself was a student at the same institution and he was active in the same intellectual milieu. These Viennese connections make it possible, and perhaps even likely, that Lowenfeld knew Riegl's published work and drew his terminology directly from it.   ¶   It is also possible, on the other hand, that Lowenfeld's terminology is not indebted directly to Riegl at all but to the sources that he and his Viennese predecessor both read – namely, the works of Johann Friedrich Herbart, Robert Vischer, Adolf von Hildebrand, and other late nineteenth-century German language writers whose neo-Kantian physiological accounts of aesthetic experience investigated the role that subjective feeling plays in conditioning the perception of form.[13] The pressing philosophical problem in Kant's day had been whether human reason was able to grasp an idealized truth behind the veil of sensory experience. The problem that these writers inherited was to account for the duality of reason and nature in the Kantian subject. In his analysis of the sublime, Kant posited the *Ding an sich* as that which lies beyond the limits of reason. In designating a certain transcendental object as something that we cannot know – the noumenon in an otherwise phenomenal world, as Karen Lang puts it – Kant departed from existing claims that nature could be entirely known and classified.[14]   ¶   To sketch a complex sequence of events quickly for the sake of the following argument, the inaugural moment for late nineteenth-century empathy theory can be located in Herbart's attempt to mediate between empiricism and rationalism.[15] Taking issue with Kant's notion of space as an a priori form of intuition, Herbart argued that the experience of space was an abstraction based on the synthesis of tactile sensations. In this process, a key role was taken up by the movement of the body, for it is only 'when one moves that the eye that sees and the hand that touches' builds up a representation of three-dimensional space.[16] Herbart's reduction of Kant's transcendental subject to a physiological interpretation of aesthetics, while highly problematic from a philosophical perspective, was widely influential, culminating in texts like Adolf Hildebrand's *Problem of Form in the Fine Arts* (1893) and terminology like Adolf Riegl's use of the haptic/optic distinction. Herbart's argument that experience of the three-dimensional world depends on supplementing visual perception with an active bodily engagement with the world made a substantial impact on the application of physiology to general theories of perception. Within the sphere of Aesthetics, writes Matthew Rampley, the conflation of the cognitive and the physiological formed the basis of empathy theory, whereby the aesthetic interest in the purely formal aspects of the object was accompanied by an emotional engagement with it.[17] ¶ In the experience of the sublime, according to Kant, the subject discovers his superiority over and above nature. For Vischer on the other hand, following Herbart and straying far from Kant's understanding of the subject as transcendental, the functions of hand and eye together were considered necessary to the experience of space and the visual perception of depth. Trading on analogies between the senses of sight and touch that ultimately originate in Aristotle's *Parva naturalia* and were developed in Late Antique and Arabic writings on the inner senses before they turn up in medieval Latin treatises on formal optics that continued to be read well into the seventeenth and even the eighteenth century, Vischer wrote of touch as the haptic sense and described seeing as 'a more subtle touching at a distance.'[18] ¶ To understand what is at stake in positing a history of art as a progression from the haptic to the optic engagement with space, as Riegl did, it is useful to bear in mind not only the physiological accounts of aesthetic experience that were new in the late nineteenth century, but also the longer history of western illusionism. The fundamental problem, recognized by artists and philosophers, lay in accounting for the unbridgeable gap between the representational field and the viewing subject. In Descartes' late work, as Lyle Massey has argued, there is increased attention to what might be called the somatic elements of perception and the idea that sensation is inextricably bound to bodies in a material sense.[19] In the mid-twentieth century, Merleau-Ponty reformulated the problem in the following clear way: to understand how perceptual activity works, we have to understand how the body works as an intertwining of vision and movement within the field of the visible. Vision is not the interior mind's eye but corporeal habitation within the sphere of contact with the world.[20] ¶ As European visual artists had long understood, there is a disjunction between how we occupy space and how we represent it.[21] Perhaps the opposition between subject and object inherent in optical naturalism – the system of illusionistic representation based on perspective – helps to explain why Riegl was interested in Vischer's Herbartian insights about 'feeling into' *(Einfühling)* forms and space.[22] In Riegl's psychology of perception, depth perception and knowledge of surfaces require a synthetic process of subjective thinking. Riegl's accompanying account of the history of artistic progress posited a new, positive role for every period of art, as exemplified in late Roman art, formerly considered a period of artistic decline.[23] Riegl described the vast interior space of the Pantheon as more purely optical and dependent on distant vision *(Fernsicht)*, therefore less haptic than its Greek and Egyptian precedents.[24] ¶ The fact that Riegl's terminology turned up in Australia three-quarters of a century later is remarkable. No matter how tentative the contact between Bardon and Riegl may have been in actual fact, attention to the intellectual heritage that encompasses them provides new insight into the effects that European theories of art history have historically produced in the world beyond Europe. The thought experiment I want to perform explores whether Riegl, still considered one of the most important theorists in the field of art history a century after his lifetime, in any way shaped the present understanding of indigenous Australian art. Geoff Bardon's encounter with the terms haptic and optic (or visual) began when he was an art student at the University of Sydney in the late 1960s, where he read Viktor Lowenfeld's *Creative and Mental Growth*, initially published in 1947.[25] Lowenfeld's text was widely adopted in courses for prospective elementary school teachers in the United States and in Australia following World War II. Like the Swiss Jean Piaget (1896–1980), whose first book on children's conceptions of the world (1928) preceded Lowenfeld's earliest publication on creativity in children by a decade, Lowenfeld adapted the pre-existing schemata of optic and haptic to his account of childhood development.[26]   ¶   For Lowenfeld, the 'haptic' and the 'visual' correspond to two types of art expression occupying opposite ends of a continuum in 'the mode of perceptual organization and the conceptual categorization of the external environment.'[27] The visually minded person engages with the environment 'primarily through the eyes and feels like a spectator,' while a person with 'haptic tendencies' is 'concerned primarily with his own body sensations and subjective experiences.'[28]   ¶   Bardon appears to have understood Lowenfeld's use of 'haptic' and 'visual' in this sense, but he did not have to account for his ideas as a systematic thinker – he was an art teacher invested in the progress of his students. Lowenfeld's description of the ideal art teacher fits Bardon exactly, judging from everything that has been reported about his encounters at Papunya, including his own autobiographical reminiscences. The new sense of self worth that emerged in the heterogeneous indigenous community of Papunya in 1971–72 was the realization of Bardon's highest aspirations as an educator.[29]   ¶   Let me emphasize that my interest is not in whether Bardon accurately understood Lowenfeld, or whether Lowenfeld's appropriation of Riegl's appropriation of Kant makes any sense to us now. [How is one person's experience more subjective than another's?] I am instead interested in the underlying discourse, specifically the recasting of prior representations in new form, like Bardon's recasting of Lowenfeld's recasting of Herbart. In this process of semiosis, as one set of connotations slides over another, what happens to manifestations of racism preserved in language?   ¶   Regarding Bardon's use of a Herbartian account of structures of seeing, at first he instructed children, but soon a group of senior men approached him with designs of their own that were then painted onto the white-washed walls of the abandoned building that came to serve as their art center (FIG 2). In all published accounts, Bardon directed the men to 'discourage all whitefella influences' in favor of painting 'their own indigenous patterns and motifs.'[30] Within months, the artists formed Papunya Tula, a professional organization, and sold their first paintings. The art education literature that underpinned Bardon's unconventional teaching practice included not only Lowenfeld, but texts by other art educators who argued that realist [*ie* western representational] art was abstract because it detached seeing from a kinesthetic engagement with one's surroundings.[31] I have already indicated the longer roots of these modernist tenets and the philosophical problem that underlies them. Bardon adapted his available sources, art education texts of the 1960s, to the circumstances at Papunya. He promoted a non-representational style that translated what *he seems to have understood* as his students' 'haptic' engagement with the world to a fully 'visual' form of painting.[32] In one sense, he reproduced problematic, essentializing distinctions between the mentalities of different people (still rooted in nineteenth-century racial ideas, though neither Riegl nor Bardon recognized this).[33] On the other hand, Bardon, like Riegl, tried to develop an understanding of art free from the racial theories of cultural evolution that they had both inherited.   ¶   There are also other contributing factors to consider, such as the extent and importance of ritual life in the western desert. As Nancy Munn's study of Warlpiri iconography (originally published in 1973) documents extensively, Aboriginal peoples of the western desert possess a highly elaborate and well defined system of representation, developed in paintings and body ornament executed in a range of natural pigments and other materials.[34] Eurocentric distinctions between the senses of sight and touch are irrelevant when one considers the highly complex interaction among the senses in any artmaking process. Developing the implications of Munn's research, linguist Jenny Green is currently documenting and analysing how closely integrated touch and sight, sound and movement [vocal/auditory and kinesic/visual modalities] are in Arandic women's sand-drawing in Central Australia:

> *The point is not the degree to which such symbols are transparent in their iconicity – there are multiple ways in which these links are made. An understanding of a multimodal event relies on a complex decoding of conventional symbols, contextual cues*

and so on. It seems to me that if we are to have an open mind about communicative systems (especially when engaging in new descriptions of very old ones) then it is important to consider all contrastive and variant aspects of the 'sensory' signal – be that sound, touch, visual material etc.[35]

Indigenous Australian storytelling provides researchers with an excellent case study of how perceptual activity works by integrating the senses within the field of movement. For this reason, the investigations of Munn and Green are also part of the legacy of nineteenth-century philosophers who sought to understand the experience of space by studying art. ¶ Unlike the anthropologists and ethnographers who studied Aboriginal systems of mark-making and visual representation before, during, and after Bardon's tenure at Papunya – who likewise collaborated with their subjects by providing them with art materials and even instructions on what to depict – Bardon the art teacher felt no qualms about engaging fully with his adult students, older initiated men. He encouraged them to paint visually coherent images that were individual, personal interpretations of the sacred, communally sanctioned designs traditionally appearing on sacred boards *(chirungas)*, as body ornamentation associated with sacred-secret ceremonies, as well as the designs I have just mentioned that were drawn in the sand to accompany the narration of stories.[36] To his great credit, Bardon carefully documented each work and did not press the artists at Papunya to reveal the esoteric significance of their paintings. Nonetheless, the untraditional use of cultural designs led to serious problems within the Aboriginal community, as Batty explains:

Indeed the designs themselves are secret and subject to complex protocols of ownership and display. Further, the rituals in which these designs are ceremonially revealed were – and still are – strictly off limits to women and children.[37]

Yet the question nags, did Riegl's structures of seeing, that is, his conception of subjective and objective engagement with the world at both the individual and collective level, have anything to do with this Australian legacy? I have already mentioned the multiple sources of the terminology that Riegl adopted. Let us now consider further what Riegl's historical scheme was meant to achieve in the broader context of nineteenth-century European debates about human cultural development. Riegl envisioned the history of art as a continuous process of development that minimized the rise and decline scheme he inherited. His objective was to eliminate Social Darwinism from the writing of art history, a subject to which he devoted some fifty pages at the beginning of his first major theoretical publication, *Stilfragen (Problems of Style)* (1893), refuting the idea of evolutionary cultural progress proposed by some of his contemporaries. In the introduction and opening chapter, where Riegl set out his theory of geometric style to refute the materialist theories of his contemporaries, he rejected theories of cultural history that posit a parallel between the physical evolution of the human race and the progress of 'civilization.' He blamed this trend on theories of racial difference that have steadily crept into the writing of art history. ¶ Riegl's objections were explicitly addressed to controversies over cultural development that extended far beyond disciplinary concerns with methodology. The fundamental issue at stake was whether racial differences in mental ability existed. Anthropological discussions in late nineteenth-century Europe and Australia, which also extended beyond scientific debates to the popular press, emphasized that aesthetic capability manifested in artistic productions helped to define the degree of cultural progress, and hence the degree of humanness.[38] The concept of art as a universal and simultaneously 'spiritual' phenomenon encompassing crafts was widely disseminated by Tylor's publications and by writings associated with the British arts and crafts movement. In this newly expanded vertical scale of cultural development, where Australian Aboriginal peoples occupied the lowest rung, most writings on Aboriginal art and culture avoided crediting indigenous Australians with any degree of creative ability.[39] ¶ Tylor and Spencer proposed basically the same arguments as Riegl, namely that all forms of human artistic production are 'spiritual' rather than 'mechanical' by nature. This conception of art as a universally human phenomenon is at the core of Riegl's revisionist concept of *Kunstwollen* and constitutes his fundamental objection to materialist theories of artistic development. Yet Riegl, like Tylor and Spencer, explicitly did not reject Darwin's theory of evolution. Indeed, who would have taken their theories of art seriously if they had objected to the dominant scientific paradigm of the day? Nor did Riegl completely reject the humanist model that granted pre-eminence to ancient Greek civilization. Again, who would have taken Riegl's theory of art seriously if, instead of explaining cultural development, he had rejected the cultural values of his day in their entirety? ¶ Lingering epistemological assumptions of cultural progress still present in Lowenfeld's text, despite his explicit acceptance of all art as equally valid, colored Bardon's practice as an art teacher when he proposed to change the 'haptic' engagement of his students to a 'visual' engagement with the world.[40] His aim was to bring dignity and prosperity to the Aboriginal community. What Bardon failed to recognize was that his understanding was ultimately grounded in a racialized view of cultural production. Furthermore, Bardon's unconditional belief in his students not withstanding, by the time Western Desert painting became an economic goldmine in the national and international art industry in the 1980s, the symbolic markings were viewed reductively within the framework of high modernist abstraction, as they still are.[41] ¶ In the process of becoming fully 'visual' art in a thoroughly western sense for their overwhelmingly white audiences, acrylic paintings from the central Western Desert negated or at least marginalized the cultural meanings that the work had for its makers and communities of origin. And this was partially by design, because the artists wanted to protect the esoteric references in their work from uninitiated viewers. More sinister are the circumstances that enable wealthy buyers and sellers to participate in the re-sale auction market, where paintings bring in sums worth hundreds of times the amount ever paid to an artist directly. At the present, none of this money benefits the artists, their descendants, or communities who produce such valuable cultural products.[42] The myths that represent indigenous Australians as hapless victims rather than active agents provide an over-simplistic account of the relocation and assimilation process practiced by the Commonwealth government.[43] Nonetheless, one unresolved question is why alcoholism and violence should be commonplace when so many highly original and successful artists emerged from Papunya and elsewhere beginning in the 1980s. The entanglement of issues of social justice and the Western Desert art movement deserves attention, demands comment and action. ¶ The romanticizing, exoticizing, and whitewashing of native artistic traditions, practices, and beliefs does not provide insight into cultural differences. Australian artists who identify with their indigenous roots who are able to critique the western art industry do exist, but what goes by the label of Aboriginal art is all too often only a mirror image of European desires.[44] Native knowledge is also increasingly lost as it is successively formatted in conformity with western values. ¶ As anthropologist Fred Myers described the situation in 2002, the circulation of acrylic paintings is not easily contained within a single regime of value – they are neither simply commodities, nor fully sacred objects.[45] As long as the question of single authorship and high art media that are still so important to the selling of art prevails, European values will provide the standard against which everyone else is judged. Aboriginal artists were configured as Australia's leading internationally known abstract artists in an astonishingly short period of time. They filled the pre-existing role of the autochthonous artist, appropriating the longstanding narrative of the male genius who recapitulates the great moments of avant-garde art without any formal education or even knowledge of the art to which the work is routinely compared.[46] Significanty, this career-making took shape in the 1980s and 90s, when formal High Modernism was passé, though of course still a profitable model in the art industry that quickly made artists like Clifford Possum and Emily Kngwarreye into international stars. While it would be callous to label them as new products on an old shelf, from the standpoint of art as a high end commodity form, that is exactly what they were – a novel twist that envigorated a tired market. ¶ Assessing Riegl's 'Australian legacy,' it should now be clear, is a complicated matter. The recursive movement of ideas shuffling between Europe and Australia over the last century that I have sketched here suggests both how individual agency can interrupt and even subvert the trans-generational reproduction of untenable, racist constructs and, concurrently, how individual agency is continually pressured by institutionally sanctioned forms of power delivered in a variety of ways. Bardon could hardly have foreseen that the forces of the art market would eventually work against the best interests of indigenous communities that he and his immediate successors tried to rehabilitate psychologically and make self-sufficient through the production and sale of art. Assumptions played out in nineteenth-century European and Australian scholarly texts were enacted by the colonial Australian government in its treatment of indigenous populations. Reverberations in the popular press and entertainment industry echoed these policies far and wide.[47] For the same reasons, however, the continuing negotiations of place and memory between different subgroups are especially clearly articulated in Australia, and worth international attention for this reason. In recent years Australia has officially begun to come to terms with its racist colonial past: when Prime Minister Kevin Rudd assumed office in January 2008, he opened Parliament with an apology to all Aboriginal people only, the second such apology offered by any government.[48] Yet, as more recent protests attest, the impoverished conditions of indigenous Australians and their unequal access to education, health services, and other rights of citizenship continue today, and racist attitudes have by no means vanished completely in Australia or elsewhere. ¶ The wider significance of the foregoing thought experiment has been to establish a long trajectory for investigating structures of seeing through the study of art. The structural intuitions of Aboriginal artists have been studied by scientists and scholars for over a century. During this time period, the cognitive and creative abilities of indigenous Australians may have been a constant factor, but appreciation has changed from considering them to be the most primitive of humans to understanding their artmaking as an exemplary manifestation of multimodal sensory integration of the body and the environment.

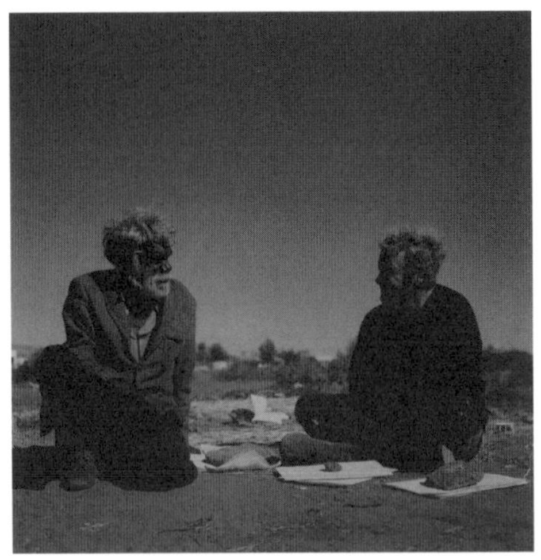

FIGURE 1 Tom Onion Tjapangati with Geoffrey Bardon, Papunya, 1973. Reproduced from Vivian Johnson, *Papunya Tula: Lives of the Artists*, 2008.

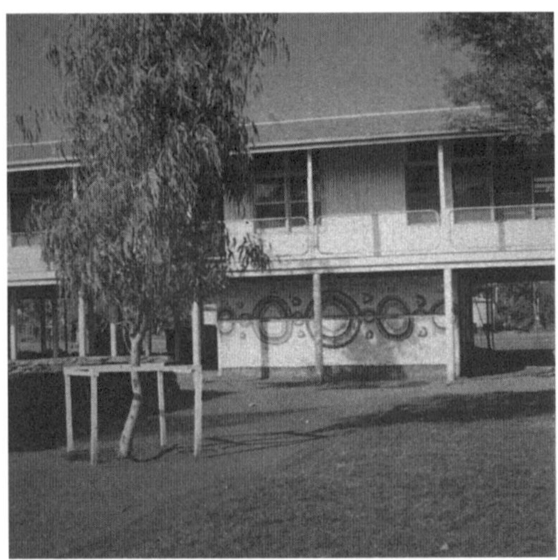

FIGURE 2 Honey Ant mural, Papunya, 1972 (since destroyed).

My deepest thanks to Philip Batty and Susan Lowish whose incisive comments on an earlier draft of this essay made me rethink the entire argument; to Kirk Ambrose and David Summers for their very helpful comments on a subsequent draft; and to Donald Preziosi for offering criticism and encouragement throughout the writing process

1.   I J McNiven and L Russell, *Appropriated Pasts: Indigenous Peoples and the Colonial Culture of Archaeology*, Altamira Press, Lanham (MD), 2005, p.49.

2.   See D Preziosi, *Brain of the Earth's Body: Art, Museums, and the Phantasms of Modernity*, University of Minnesota Press, Minneapolis, 2003, pp.133–35, for a related discussion of the Pitt Rivers Museum, with further references.

3.   Although Spencer was an evolutionist, his partner Frank Gillen had a much greater respect for the creative powers of Aboriginal peoples. A large number of professional anthropologists now work on behalf of Aboriginal claimants for Aboriginal organizations such as the Central Land Council.

4.   D Tacey, *Edge of the Sacred: Transformation in Australia*, Harper Collins, Melbourne, 1995, p.129, cited by Lowish, 'Writing on Aboriginal Art', p.163.

5.   The idea precedes nineteenth-century social evolutionism, to which Spencer and Tylor are both indebted, originating in classical antiquity and elaborated during the Renaissance and Enlightenment eras. According to the theory known as 'Antiquation,' Aboriginals were variants of Neanderthals and therefore the equivalent of prehistoric Europeans. McNiven and Russell, *Appropriated Pasts*, p.39.

6.   See discussion by E Willis, 'The production of Aboriginal states': Australian Aboriginal and settler exhibits at the Paris Universal Exhibition of 1855,' in *Seize the Day: Exhibitions, Australia and the World*, K Darian-Smith, R Gillespie, C Jordan and E Willis (eds.), Monash University Press, Melbourne, 2008, pp.82–102, with further references.

7.   The historical emergence of Aboriginal painting as a respected art form is far more complex than this brief narrative can suggest. See H Morphy, *Aboriginal Art*, Phaidon, London, 1998; and idem, *Becoming Art: Exploring Cross-cultural Categories*, Berg, Oxford–New York, 2007. By the 1960s, in the Northern Territory, bark painting was a well established genre within the art industry (see Morphy, 'A Short History of Yolnu Art,' in *Becoming Art*, pp. 27–86, with further references).

8.   Personal communication with Philip Batty, February 5, 2009.

9.   *Old Masters of the Western Desert*, forthcoming exhibition curated by J Ryan and P Batty, September-December 2011, National Gallery of Victoria, Melbourne.

10.   A Stoler, *Race and the Education of Desire: Foucault's History of Sexuality and the Colonial Order of Things*, 1995.

11.   Citing Stoler, *Race and the Education of Desire*, p.204.

12.   A D Efland, 'Viktor Lowenfeld' in *Education Encyclopedia*, accessed on-line at: http://www.answers.com/topic/viktor-lowenfeld, on February 22, 2009.

13.   M Rampley, 'From Symbol to Allegory: Aby Warburg's Theory of Art', *Art Bulletin* 77 (1995), pp.41–55.

14.   K Lang, 'The Dialectics of Decay: Rereading the Kantian Subject', *The Art Bulletin* 79 (September 1997) pp.413–39, citing p.422.

15.   My summary follows Rampley, 'From Symbol to Allegory' pp.45–47.

16.   Citing Rampley, 'From Symbol to Allegory' p.45.

17.   Rampley, 'From Symbol to Allegory' p.46.

18.   Robert Vischer, 'On the Optical Sense of Form' p.97.

19. L Massey, *Picturing Space, Displacing Bodies: Anamorphosis in Early Modern Theories of Perspective*, Pennsylvania State University Press, University Park (PA), 2007.

20. As cited by Massey, *Picturing Space*, p.103.

21. Massey, *Picturing Space*, p.108, on Cezanne's doubt – that is, his lifelong project of trying not to copy but to fully inhabit his perception of nature.

22. Iverson, *Aloïs Riegl*, pp.75–76, argues that Riegl's intermediary was Adolf von Hildebrand, whose *Das Problem der Form in der bildenden Kunst [The Problem of Form in the Visual Arts]*, appeared in 1893, the same year as Riegl's Stilfragen.

23. Vasari wrote about the grotesques of the late Augustan to Titus era (c.80 ACE) as manifestations of a period of decline, in keeping with the opinions of Vitruvius.

24. The term Einfühling was already used by Robert Vischer's more famous father Friedrich-Theodor Vischer, regarding architectural form. See Rampley, 'From Symbol to Allegory.'

25. According to Efland, 'Viktor Lowenfeld,' in *Creative and Mental Growth* 'became the single most influential textbook in art education during the latter half of the twentieth century.' For Bardon's knowledge of Lowenfeld, see P Carter, 'Introduction: The Interpretation of Dreams' in *Papunya: A Place Made After the Story: The Beginnings of the Western Desert Painting Movement*, University of Melbourne Miegunyah Press Melbourne, (2004), 2007, xvii–xviii.

26. J Piaget, et al., *Judgment and Reasoning in the Child*, London, K. Paul, Trench, Trubner & Co. ltd., Harcourt, Brace and Company, New York, 1928, took up the formation of haptic and optic schemas in his account of childhood intelligence. V Lowenfeld, *The Nature of Creative Activity*, Harcourt Brace, New York, 1939.

27. Lowenfeld and Brittain, *Creative and Mental Growth*, 5th ed., The Macmillan Company, New York, 1970, p.234 (subsequent citations are to this edition).

28. Lowenfeld, *Creative and Mental Growth*, pp.234–5.

29. The euphoria was shortlived, however. Although this history is the subject of new research by Philip Batty and Judith Ryan (see n.9), the current understanding is that soon the participating artists were accused by their own friends and relatives of revealing sacred-secret 'men's business' without sanction to women and children and to the non-indigenous public. As a result of serious disagreements within the community, painting activities were interrupted, for nearly fifteen years in some places. See J Ryan with G Bardon, *Mythscapes: Aboriginal Art of the Desert from the National Gallery of Victoria*, The Gallery, Melbourne, 1989; G Bardon and J Bardon, *Papunya: The Place; Papunya Tula: Genesis and Genius*, H. Perkins and H.Fink (eds.), Art Gallery of New South Wales in association with Papunya Tula artists, Sydney, 2000. Meanwhile Bardon was accused by his government employers of subverting his educational mission in introducing profit motives and accused by the artists of being complicit with the art galleries and otherwise selling them out. Bardon suffered a nervous breakdown in 1972 from which he never fully recovered, due to the disastrous psychiatric care that he received in Sydney which left him physically and mentally debilitated, contributing to his premature death in 2003 at the age of 63. The story of Geoffrey Bardon's life is the subject of a documentary film, Mr. Patterns, directed by Catriona McKenzie, produced by Nic Testoni et al, Lindfield, New South Wales, Film Australia, 2004.

30. Bardon, cited in Carter, 'Introduction: The Interpretation of Dreams,' xviii.

31. Cited in Carter, 'Introduction: The Interpretation of Dreams,' xvii, citing Lowenfeld, in *Creative and Mental Growth*, p.261.

32. As Carter, 'Introduction: The Interpretation of Dreams,' has already emphasized.

33. See further, my 'Vision Itself Has Its History', 'Race,' Nation, and Renaissance Art History', in *Reframing the Renaissance: Art and Visual Culture in Europe and Latin America 1450–1650*, Yale University Press, London-New Haven, 1995, pp.78–81.

34. N D Munn, *Walpiri Iconography: Graphic Representation and Cultural Symbolism in a Central Australian Society*, Cornell University Press, Ithaca-New York, 1973.

35. Jenny Green, personal communication with the author, November 2, 2008. Green is currently completing her dissertation on this subject at the University of Melbourne entitled *Between the Earth and the Air: Multimodality in Arandic Sand Stories*.

36. See Munn, *Walpiri Iconography*.

37. Batty, personal communication Feb 5, 2009.

38. Darwin placed savages at a point intermediary between man and animals – and even lower than some animals: 'Judging from the hideous ornaments and the equally hideous music admired by most savages, it might be argued that their aesthetic faculty was not so highly developed as in certain animals, for instance in birds.' ('The Descent of Man and Selection in Relation to Sex', I, pp.64, as cited by N Stepan, *The Idea of Race in Science: Great Britain 1800–1960*, London-Basingstoke, Macmillan Press and Hamden (CT), Archon Books, 1982, p.54.

39. See S Lowish, *Writing on Aboriginal Art 1802–1929: A Critical and Cultural analysis of the Construction of a Category*, Ph.D, dissertation, Monash Unviersity, 2004, especially p.123.

40. Carter, 'Introduction,' xviii.

41. See F Myers, *Painting Culture: The Making of an Aboriginal High Art*, Duke University Press, Durham, 2002.

42. N De Marchi, 'The Impact of Opportunistic Dealers on Sustainability in the Australian Aboriginal Desert Paintings Market,' paper presented at the International Congress of the History of Art, *Cross-Cultural Migrations*, Melbourne University, Melbourne, revised February 22, 2009.

43. An account of the historical circumstances leading to the establishment of Papunya is offered by Philip Batty: 'The records actually show that Aboriginal people chose to leave the bush themselves and the establishment of Papunya represented an attempt by government to deal with this exodus' (personal communication, Feb 5, 2009). See also *Colliding Worlds: First Contact in the Western Desert 1932–1984*, Philip Batty (ed.), Museum Victoria and the National Aboriginal Cultural Institute Tandonya, Melbourne, 2006.

44. Citing P. Batty, 'Selling Emily: Confessions of a White Art Advisor,' ms, p.6. See also, P Batty, 'White Redemption Rituals', in *Moving Anthropology: Critical Indigenous Studies*, E T Lea et al, Charles Darwin University Press, Darwin, 2006.

45. Myers, *Painting Culture*,

46. See for example, M Neale, 'Marks of Meaning: The Genius of Emily Kame Kngawarreye,' in *Emily Kame Kngwarreye: Utopia, The Genius of EKK*, exh cat., National Museum of Australia and National Museum of Art, Osaka, 2008, pp.33–51.

47. On nineteenth-century world fairs at the beginning of this history, see *Seize the Day: Exhibitions, Australia, and the World*, especially the essay by Willis, 'The production of Aboriginal states.'

48. A formal apology for historical injustice to native peoples was offered by the Canadian government in 1998. See SBS, *The First Australians*, accessed at http://www.sbs.com.au/firstaustralians/index/index/epid/7, for footage of the Parliament session. Leading up to the Rudd's apology, in 1992, the highest court of Australia ruled in favor of Eddie Koiki Mabo's fight for Australian law to recognize that his people own Murray Island, thus finally overturning the colonial notion of *terra nullius*, that the land belonged to no one before the time of white settlement.

Sir Harry Kroto

Art & science: geodesy in materials science

This article is in honour of the outstanding efforts made by Martin Kemp in eliminating the cultural barrier between the arts and the sciences and in so doing making a major contribution to enlightened general education. This text particularly focuses on the way creative activity initiated primarily by 'artistic' motives can result, serendipitously, in an important scientific advance.

Introduction

In 1988 Ken McKay and I carried out, primarily for fun, a fascinating little project which inadvertently made a major contribution to our understanding of carbon particles whose structures at nanoscale dimensions had heretofore been impossible to understand. Although several attempts had been made over many years they had resulted in quite erroneous conclusions which ended up being accepted for several decades.[1]

Geodesic Domes

After the Fullerenes had been discovered[2] I thought, in the late 1980s, it might be neat to build my own mini-Buckminster Fuller Dome (like the one pictured in FIGURE 1 but a little smaller!) and purchased molecular modelling kits to do it. There was no thought at the time that this was a research project – it was just a fun project to build a large beautiful model to display essentially like a sculpture in our laboratory. The image of Buckminster Fuller's famous Dome at the Montreal Expo 1967 shown in FIGURE 1 is from Graphis 1967. ¶ The original little fun project with Ken McKay led us first to some fascinating work by the mathematicians Goldberg and Coxeter on what are now called Goldberg polyhedra. When the models were constructed, much to my surprise they were not smoothly spherical like the dome above. I had assumed this would be the case from my cursory perusal of the images of all the domes I had seen. Instead each model that we constructed (cf FIG 2A and FIG 2B) was essentially a closed icosahedral monosurface consisting of a hexagonal network of struts that swept from one, of 12, pentagonal cusps to another. ¶ I

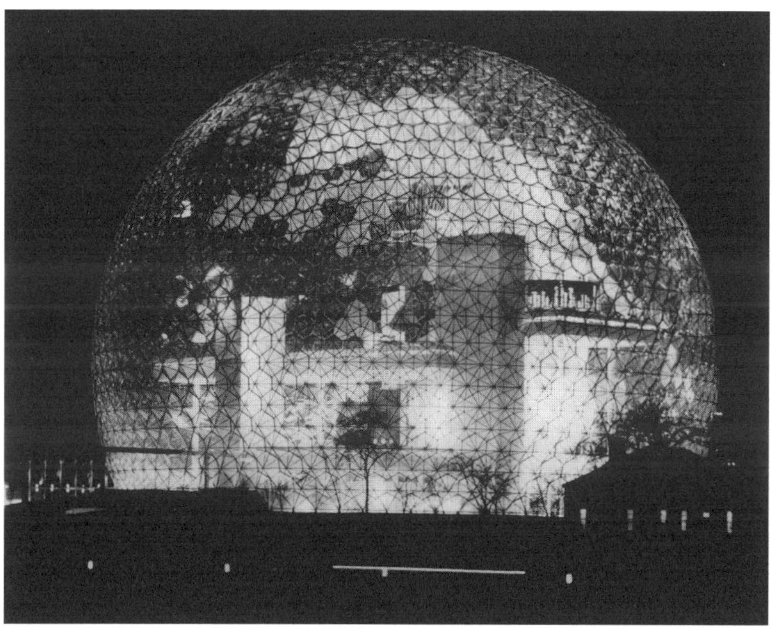

FIGURE 1 Photograph of the Buckminster Fuller's Dome at the Montreal Expo 1967.

remember being quite perplexed at the time as to why the models were not spheroidal as I had expected. Then I returned to study images of Fuller's domes much more carefully and realised that although the hexagons were in general fairly symmetric those in the neighbourhood of the pentagons were quite distorted as can be seen in FIG 3. ¶ Then I realised that I (and apparently everyone else) had overlooked something that had been under our noses in the literature for years. I had looked at electron microscope images of spheroidal carbon particles several times in the past and only now realised what I must have been looking at. Several years earlier

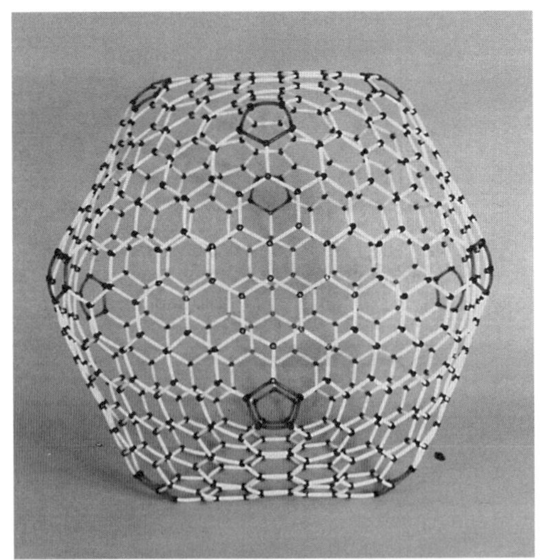

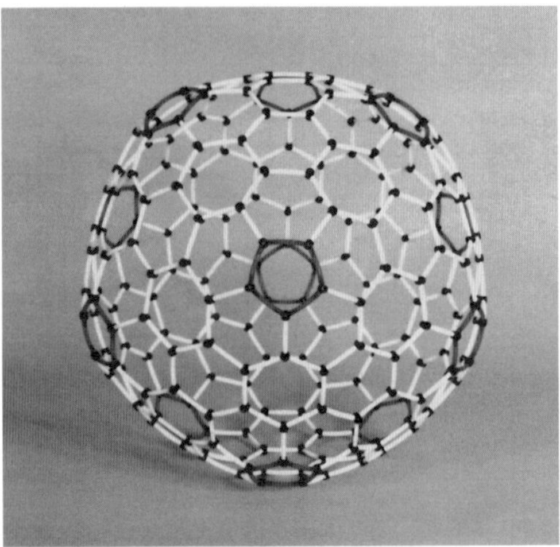

FIGURE 2 A (above) and **FIGURE B** (below) Photographs of molecular models of the Giant Fullerenes C_{240} and C_{540}. The models were based on the Goldberg polyhedra. Notice that as the cages become larger the icosahedral symmetry of the structure becomes more and more obvious as the overall shape becomes less spheroidal and more polyhedral.

high resolution electron microscope images of onion-like structures had been published by Sumio Iijima. A typical example of these elegant images is shown in FIG 4 where a picture taken by Daniel Ugarte is depicted. The electron microscope yields an image that can be considered as a sort of cross-section of the spheroidal particle that actually consists of concentric spheroidal shells, much like an onion. Thus one can effectively get an image of the structure that one has effectively sliced into two

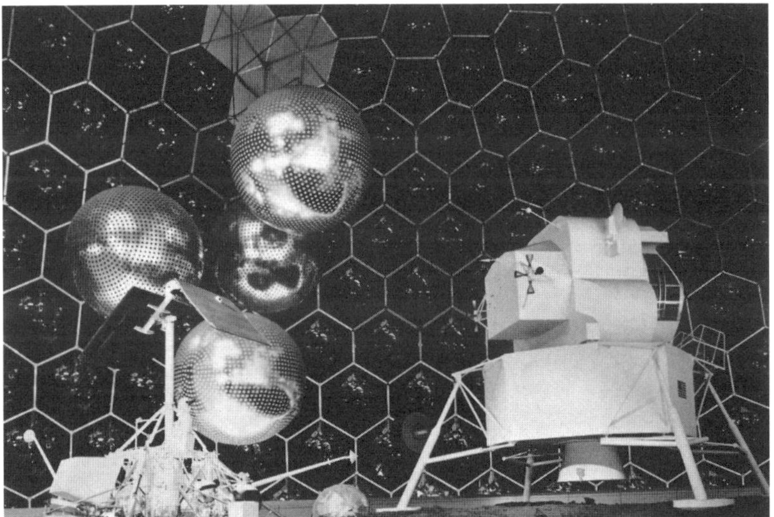

Two images taken from inside the Expo 67 Dome. **FIGURE 3 A** (above) A photograph was published in Graphis 43 (1967) and **FIGURE 3 B** (overleaf) was taken by Robin Whyman who kindly gave me a copy of his slide. By great good fortune these photographs which are of the first US space capsule and an Eagle Moon Lander replica also both show a pentagon. Particularly interesting from the science/art point of view is the asymmetry of the hexagons which abut the pentagons. This distortion was necessary to produce the near spheroidal structure of the Expo67 Dome. The Giant Fullerenes possesses their own unique quasi-icosahedral 'Giant Fullerene' shapes consisting of relatively smooth surfaces which sweep between the 12 pentagonal cusps necessary for closure of each Fullerene.

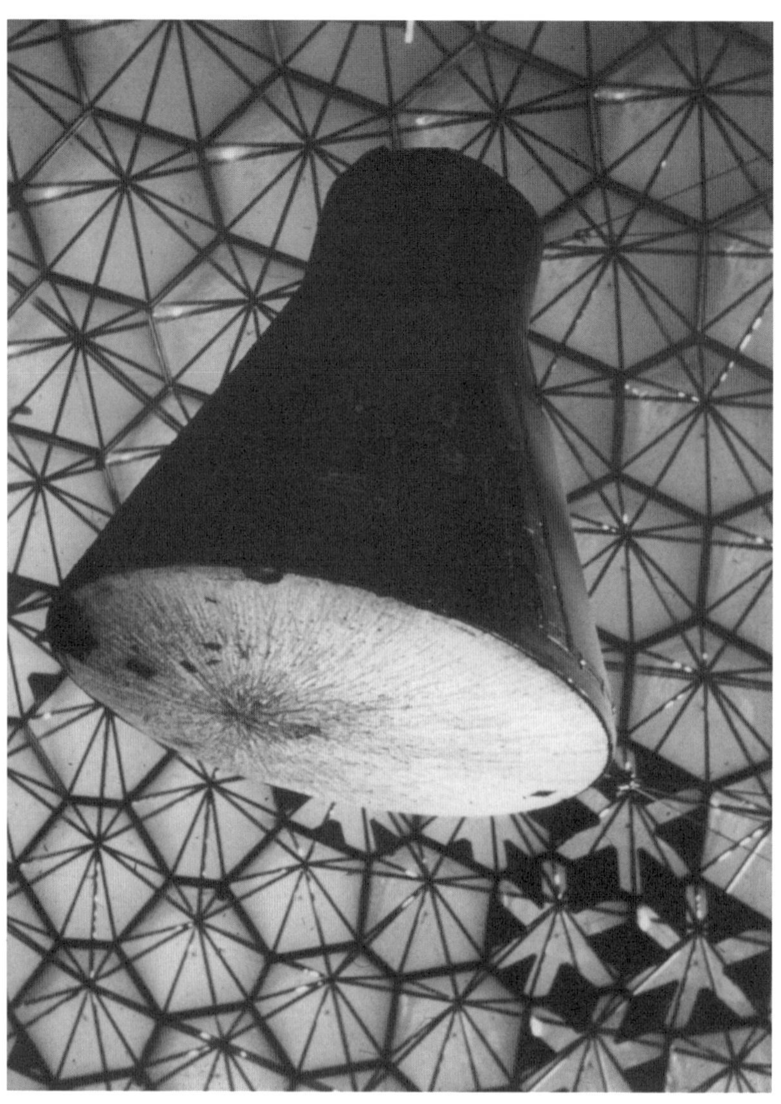

hemispheres to reveal the inner structure, much as cutting horizontally through a tree trunk reveals tree rings. What I realised was that I and others had missed the fact that the rings were not quite circular but possessed subtle curvature variations which betrayed the fact that they were actually quasi-icosahedral as were our Giant Fullerene models. I had seen what I wanted to see rather than what was actually there. To find quantitative confirmation of this conjecture Ken wrote a computer programme to create a set of Giant Fullerenes of ever increasing size FIG 4. The cages were then placed one inside the other as shown in FIG 5.

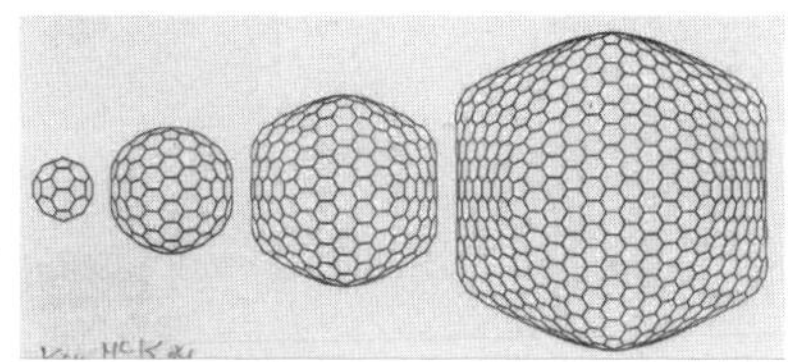

FIGURE 4 Set of Giant Fullerenes of gradually increasing size.

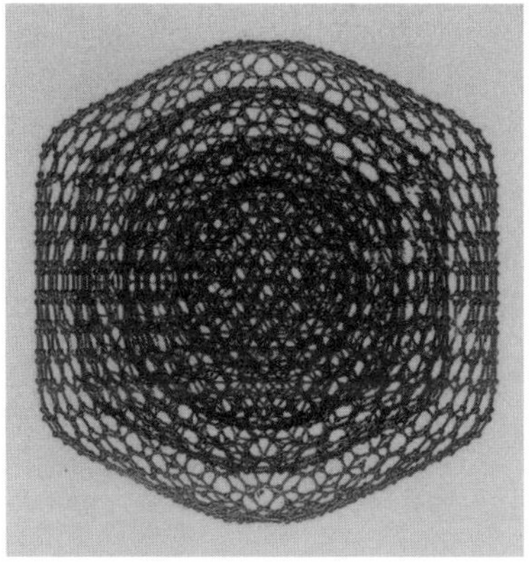

FIGURE 5 Schematic diagram depicting four Fullerene Cages in an onion-like concentric arrangement.

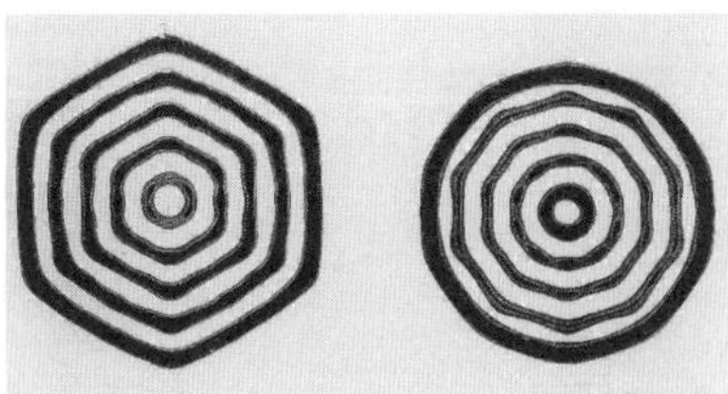

FIGURE 6 A and B Simulated high resolution electron microscope images of a carbon particle consisting of 5 concentric Fullerene cages seen along two different axes; A The left hand image shows 6-fold symmetry whereas B The right hand image shows 10-fold symmetry.

In an electron microscope a beam of electrons is passed through an object and if the beam encounters an array of atoms which possess some phase relation as they do when the electrons pass along a channel in which a graphite wall lies, then the electrons may be diffracted and a dark line appears in the resulting pattern cf FIG 6A and 6B. One then observes what is effectively a cross section of the particle. The Fullerenes tend to show polygons with something between 6 fold and 10 fold symmetry. Of course perfect icosahedral symmetry is very unlikely but flattening should be, and is, quite common FIG 7 and FIG 8.

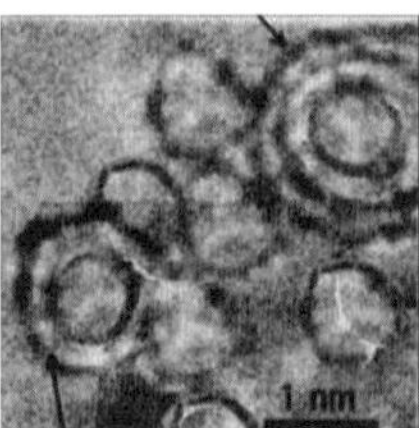

FIGURE 7 Actual high resolution electron microscope spheroidal carbon particle consisting of only two shells. The hexagonal shape of the outer shell is very clear and is totally consistent with the simulation shown in FIG 6. Image from Mordkovich and Endo.

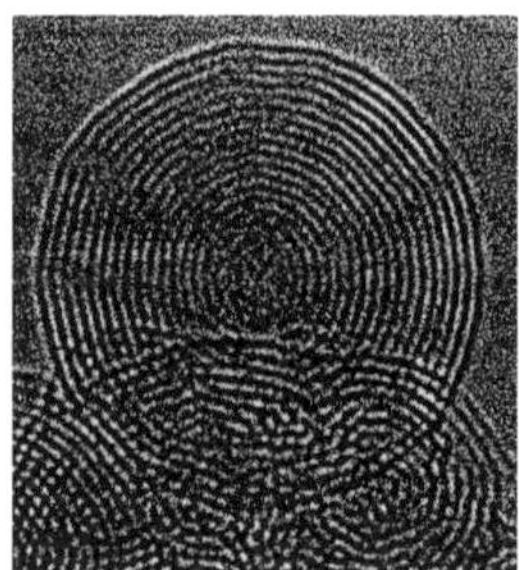

FIGURE 8 Actual high resolution electron microscope spheroidal carbon particle consisting of only two shells. The hexagonal shape of the outer shell is very clear and is totally consistent with the simulation shown in Fig 6. Image from Mordkovich and Endo.

Conclusion

In this article an account is given of a project which was originally initiated to satisfy the aesthetic creative impulse to build a 3-dimensional model or sculpture based on a molecular structural recipe. In the event the resulting model turned out to have some unique and unexpected shape characteristics which led to further scientific investigation that explained some important nanoscale structural observations that had been seen many years beforehand and mistakenly explained. The account is a rare example of artistic creativity resulting in a key scientific advance.

I wish to thank Ken McKay and David Wales my colleagues in the original scientific investigation and Daniel Ugarte and Morinobu Endo for their electron microscope and their images.

1.   H W Kroto and K McKay, 'The Formation of Quasi-icosahedral Spiral Shell Carbon Particles' *Nature*, 331, 1988, pp.328–331.

2.   H W Kroto, J R Heath, S C O'Brien, R F Curl and R E Smalley, 'C_{60}: Buckminsterfullerene', *Nature*, 318 (No.6042), 1985, pp.162–163.

Tony Robbin

The fourth dimension in painting

In 1983 art historian Linda Henderson[1] proposed, and now many agree, that the secret inspiration for twentieth century art was four-dimensional geometry. At one propitious moment, a serious and sophisticated engagement with the geometric fourth dimension pushed Pablo Picasso (1881–1973) and his collaborators into the discovery of Cubism. These artists used the new four-dimensional geometry to structure new perceptions and make their emotional experience whole.   ¶   Although taken by many at the time to be just another example of Fauvism, Picasso's *Portrait d'Ambroise Vollard,* Spring 1910, is not Fauve in spirit or execution. The subject is not a generic noble savage, but a specific person – the portrait of the distinguished (and pompous) art dealer Ambroise Vollard, a leading proponent of Fauvism and one of Picasso's early supporters. There is an exaggeration of color in the portrait, but it does not have an expressionist aim. In fact there is a de-saturation of color. Rather than Van Gogh's self-described 'emotion of an ardent temperament,' there is a cool analysis of space, but certainly not the cylinders, cubes, and cones that Cézanne would have recognized. According to art historian Palau i Fabre,[2] this painting was very important to Picasso, and he worked on it for months. Detached from his earlier sources, Picasso must have found a new inspiration, a missing link. Henderson compared the *Vollard* to a figure in Esprit Jouffret's *Traité élémentaire de géométrie à quatre dimensions* (1903). She found in Picasso's faceted and disintegrating figure a close resemblance to Jouffret's illustration, and she admirably documented the full presence of the fourth dimension in the popular imagination in Europe and the United States at the turn of the twentieth century.   ¶   But if Picasso had left it at that, Cubism would not have developed into the consciousness-expanding force that it became. Six months later, in the fall of 1910, Picasso's *Portrait of Henry Kahnweiler* was as big a departure from the vision and philosophy of the *Vollard* as the

Vollard had been from Picasso's earlier work. While the *Vollard* is, in effect, an exploded technical drawing of planes, the *Kahnweiler* is composed of multiple transparent, interpenetrating cubes that cannot be brought together. Multiple cubes make up the head rather than a single cube defining it, and even taken all together, the head seems incomplete. Rectilinear cells are again seen in the torso, the still life, and the background, showing the programmatic nature of the spatial analysis in the painting. ¶ One way to understand the difference between the *Vollard* and *Kahnweiler* heads is to consider the now-forgotten pedagogic technique for teaching Cubism to painting students: students were instructed first to sculpt a head in clay and then to whack it with a piece of lumber to 'find the planes,' to facet the modeled clay. The technique could well produce an image like the *Vollard*, but it could never render an image close to the *Kahnweiler*, with its aggressive manipulation of interpenetrating volumes. ¶ It is fitting that when Picasso made his most important conceptual breakthrough, it was with a portrait of Kahnweiler. Among Picasso's several dealers and patrons at that time, it was Kahnweiler that the young Picasso trusted, Kahnweiler who was Picasso's banker, Kahnweiler who went into Picasso's studio in his absence to gather Picasso's materials for him and to take away finished work, Kahnweiler to whom Picasso sent his most difficult paintings. Young, intellectual, foreign (German-Jewish), and scrappy, Kahnweiler would make his reputation with the new art of Cubism, Vollard's exhibitions of Fauvism having already become the establishment. Picasso formed strong bonds with a number of colleagues in his youth, mostly male painters and critics; Kahnweiler seems to have been the only dealer in this select group. ¶ Picasso's new idea of space in the *Kahnweiler* is explained by looking more deeply into Jouffret's text and understanding the methods found in it. In *Traité*, Jouffret uses four illustrations of a four-dimensional cube, a hypercube, to demonstrate four different techniques for visualizing the fourth dimension. Close examination of these illustrations reveals a striking similarity to the techniques used by Picasso in the *Kahnweiler*, specifically the head (FIG 1). Jouffret shows the eight separate three-dimensional cells of the hypercube blown out; these are the sections, or three-dimensional slices, of the hypercube taken along the coordinate axes. The advantage of this method is that the cells are not distorted by perspective projection, and all are revealed. Additionally, the close proximity of their common vertices makes their reassembly in the fourth dimension easier to imagine. ¶ Next is Jouffret's development of four-dimensional mechanical drawing. Jouffret imagined the hypercube to be inside a glass box, and the image that is visible through each pane of glass sticks on that pane (like a daguerreotype) as the glass box is unfolded and laid flat. There are six pairings of four axes, labeled X_1, X_2, X_3, and X_4 (some planes have an edge in common, some only a point in common), and so there are six glass planes on the circumscribing box. This technique shows the apparent rotation of the figure from different angles. This technique is clearly visible in *Kahnweiler*: the cube of Kahnweiler's face is rotated 45 degrees to the cube of Kahnweiller's head. Such rotation could only have been inspired by Jouffret. When I presented this material to Martin Kemp's students, art historian Frederika Adam pointed out a further similarity: Kahnweiler's hair resembles the curved directional arrows in the Jouffret drawing. ¶ Jouffret also uses the projective model, where seven cells of the hypercube are shown nested inside an eighth. This drawing shows the progression from point to hypercube: a point is moved one unit length to make a line, the line is moved perpendicular to itself to make a square, the square is slid back to make a cube, and finally the cube is extruded into the fourth dimension to make a hypercube. The smaller cube only appears to be inside the larger; it is actually behind it, in the fourth dimension, farther away from the viewer and drawn in four-to-three perspective projection. Projected to three-space, all the cells are in the same space at the same time. ¶ Electrified by the pictures in *Traité*, Picasso must have also read the text and understood the mathematical point made by a fourth illustration: Jouffret's nonperspective projection of a hypercube. The figure is rotated so that no cells are hidden, and the ones behind are noted with dotted lines. Here again, we can see cubes nested within cubes that are usefully compared to the *Kahnweiler*. But the accompanying text makes a different point that is also relevant to a full understanding of the *Kahnweiler's* originality: Jouffret argues that that the boundary of the hypercube is composed of three-dimensional cells. No two-dimensional surface is a skin of a four-dimensional cube any more than rods connecting the corners of a cube are a skin that fully encloses that cube. The odd way in which spaces are both inside and outside a four-dimensional figure is the subject of both Jouffret's illustration and Picasso's portrait of Kahnweiler. For seven hundred years Western painters have been concerned with the skin of objects: how light reflects off the surface, how the surface defines volume. The four-dimensional projection model freed Picasso from the tyranny of the surface, and that eventually allowed him to fully present psychological portraits of the people in his life. ¶ The *Kahnweiler*, then, brought Cubism to its full realization; it was a formulation that, for the first time, clearly distinguished Cubism from Fauvism. The powerful intellectual achievement of lasting influence that started with the *Vollard* and ended with the *Kahnweiler* could only have come from a consideration of the Jouffret text, and especially of the images discussed above. Only with the *Kahnweiler* did Picasso fully engage four-dimensional geometry to make it his own. By focusing his attention on the hypercube, he was able to discover the cubes in Cubism. Perhaps is should be called Hypercubism instead of Cubism. ¶ Picasso's private application of four-dimensional geometry to a formal issue in painting would have interested his colleagues, but why should it have such resonance with the public? According to Henderson[3] in her essay *Modernism and Science*, Röntgen's publication of his findings at the end of December 1895 triggered the most immediate and widespread reaction to a scientific discovery before the mid-twentieth-century explosion of the first atomic bomb. The ability to see through clothing and flesh to the skeleton offered a startling new view of living beings. X-rays made solid matter transparent, revealing previously invisible forms and suggesting a new, more fluid relationship of those forms to the space around them. That lesson was not lost on Cubist and Futurist painters, who adopted a similar transparency and fluidity in their approach to form. 'Who can still believe in the opacity of bodies?' the Italian Futurist painter Umberto Boccioni queried in his *Technical Manifesto of Futurist Painting* of April 1910. (Henderson, 2005) ¶ With the discovery of x-rays, science proved that visible light, being only one small part of the electromagnetic spectrum, did not reveal all the truth there is to 'see,' and specifically that there was a world of visual information behind the opaque surface of things.   ¶   Before Cubism, Western painting relied exclusively on the external appearance of things: how the light on a surface depicted three-dimensional form, how light reflecting off different surfaces communicated the texture of these surfaces, and how these three-dimensional surfaces blocked out three-dimensional space. But in 1910, Picasso became the champion of a new culture that was told by science that the essence of things lay in structures that skin hid. Picasso's private use of the fourth dimension – specifically the projection model – spoke to so many, then and now, because it accomplished a goal of the whole culture. The projection method of modeling four-dimensional space puts more than one three-dimensional space in the same place at the same time; no two-dimensional surface can encompass this space. Cubism was no vacuous formal improvisation; it rocked Western painting because it offered a new way of seeing space that was considered to be truer to life. Picasso used the technical drawing of four-dimensional geometry to show his audience the reality they knew existed but could not otherwise see.   ¶   As Henderson has discovered, the fourth dimension (especially understood as four-dimensional geometry) has inspired and influenced artists in every generation since Picasso used it to invent Cubism. New since Picasso's time, computer graphics has greatly enhanced our ability to see and work with four–dimensional objects. My own artwork is fully based on the visualization of four-dimensional space. In close consultation and collaboration with world-famous mathematicians for 35 years, (Tom Banchoff, chair emeritus of the mathematics department at Brown University, Scott Carter, chair of the mathematics department at the University of South Alabama, at Mobile, George Francis, distinguished professor of mathematical visualization at the University of Illinois, Urbana) I have come to a sophisticated understanding of four-dimensional geometry, written pioneering programs to visualize four-dimensional figures, and brought that knowledge and experience to my art.   ¶   Following the ideas wherever they led, I passed through five periods, each with its own formal strategy and its own artform. These formal innovations bring the viewer to a new way of seeing by exploring the ways in which the fourth dimension is brought to our three-dimensional world. ¶ 1 Putting the viewer in more than one place at one time. In these early paintings, five linear patterns are superimposed at different angles to the picture plane; the viewer is above, to the left, to the right etc of a background structure that itself is made of reversing figures. Further patterns are sprayed through stencils to create a complex space, rich in color and texture. One focuses on a pattern and senses a location in space, only to be (psychologically) displaced when focusing on a second pattern, and so on. Eventually the viewer sees two or more patterns at once. It is as if a trained listener, on hearing a fugue, keeps track of the several melodic lines running forward and backward even when the notes are presented as chords. Associated with Pattern Painting at the time, these paintings were mainly dispersed to European collectors. ¶ 2 and 3 Planar rotation: This unique, quicksilver property of four-dimensional space is essential to an understanding of four-dimensional space: One can rotate a page around a pin-point, or a box around an axle; in four dimensions one can rotate an object around a plane. Here, four-dimensional rigid structures appear to flex and turn inside out in the same way that shadows of ordinary objects stretch and flex when moved. First seen in computer visualizations, planar rotation was brought to life in a series of relief artwoks from 1981 to 1989. I discovered that using two-dimensional elements, painted lines, and three dimensional elements, structures made of rods, planar rotation could be generated as the viewer passes by the artwork. In a further development, the two-dimensional elements became the cast shadows of the three-dimensional elements: the relief structures were lit by a red light and a blue light. Where the lights shined together there was white on the wall, but sharp, intensely colored red lines and blue lines were also made by the lights. 3D glasses could be worn for a further view of these works that replicated four-dimensional rotation. Original and magical, major works of these two types were exhibited in the IBM Gallery in New York, and at the McNay Museum in San Antonio, and many commercial and university galleries. ¶ 4 Quasicrystals. Neither crazy quilts nor regular rigid patterns, quasicrystal are non-repeating patterns (an apparent contradiction in terms) with remarkable, new visual properties that were discovered by mathematicians only recently, and are related to higher-dimensional lattices. I worked five years to create a quasicrystal sculpture for the Danish Technical University. Large enough to be architecture, the structure appeared to change its structure from triangles, to squares, to five-pointed stars depending on one's orientation inside, and the shadows the rigid structure cast also had 2-fold, 3-fold, and 5-fold symmetry depending on the position of the sun. Transparent acrylic plates in the structure create a kaleidoscope of color. Many quasicrystal models and temporary structures were also made and exhibited (FIG 6). With my consultation and using my programs, George Francis and his students installed the first virtual-environment quasicrystal at the Beckman Institute, and this cutting edge mathematical research is continuing. Francis is also working to recreate my Denmark sculpture in his virtual environment facility – the CUBE.　¶　5 Four-dimensional Topology and the space of Special Relativity. One can tie a (one-dimensional) string in a knot because it can pass through the third dimension to overlap and underlay itself: two more dimensions than the string itself. To do the same with a two-dimensional object such as a sheet, one needs access to four dimensions. Since 1995 and especially since 2000 when I renewed my friendship with Scott Carter, I have been knotting and braiding multiple three-dimensional spaces in five-dimensional space; this is the space-on-space of Special Relativity. Paintings that initially resemble my early paintings resulted. In these new works, however, three-dimensional spaces are established by linear lattices that flow over and under each other and, paradoxically through each other, as what is logical in higher-dimensional space becomes paradoxical when projected to three-space. The viewer becomes comfortable with these paradoxes and uses them to see the higher-dimensional space in that same way we can see a regular cube from its distorted, rubbery and illogical two dimensional shadow. Transparencies of color help to flip the space and establish the higher-dimensional visualizations (FIG 7 & 8).　¶　A few years ago I realized that each of these approaches investigated a different property of four-dimensional *projection*. I had been introduced to the computer visualization of the hypercube by Tom Banchoff's classic film *The Hypercube: Slicings and Projections,* which clearly showed the difference between these two approaches: slicings are three-dimensional stacked layers, whereas projections are shadows of the whole figure. In common usage concerning three-dimensional figures, projections are the norm (show a chair on a piece of paper), but because four-dimensional geometry is often confused with its application to spacetime physics, people usually think of it as space slices in a progression of time units. However, the true lesson of physics is that we should be thinking in terms of projections: relativistic spacetimes are related to one another by projection operators, and quantum multiplicities of causality and history are also modeled in projective spaces. The space of the studio in which I am writing may be usefully thought of as a slice of spacetime, and the studio can be imagined to be as big as the country, the earth, the inner solar system. But space is much larger than that: the galaxy, the cluster, the whole universe. And space is much smaller than the studio: a few molecules of air, their atoms, quarks and gluons, spin networks. Space is a slice only in the tiny part of this spectrum that we live in; in all the rest it is a projection. These ideas are further expounded in my book *Shadows of Reality, The Fourth Dimension in Relativity, Cubism, and Modern Thought.* ¶ *The Fourth Dimension* has always connoted power over complexity – an architecture to house the multiplicity of spaces that increasingly are part of modern life. Both the objective space of physics and the subjective space of personal experience require a richer structure than a mere three-dimensional geometry can provide. I have been proud to be a part of this consciousness-expanding program in my geometry research and especially in my art.

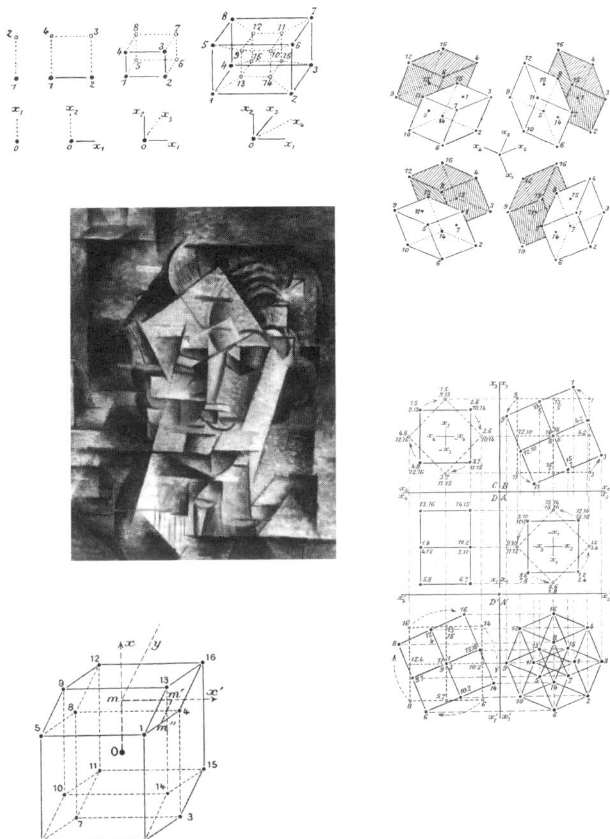

FIGURE 1 (centre left) Picasso's *Portrait of Henry Kahnweiler* (1910) is not faceted; rather, it is composed of many interpenetrating cubes (as shown here in a detail of the head). **FIGURE 2–5** (Clockwise from top left) Jouffret's 1903 illustrations. The generation of a hypercube from a line, including a perspective drawing of a hypercube in which cells in the distance are shown smaller and thus appear to be inside. An exploded drawing of the cells of a hypercube. Jouffret's mechanical drawing of a hypercube using the glass box approach. An isometric drawing of a hypercube, in which rear cells are shown to be the same size as cells in the foreground; this last image figure accompanies a discussion of the boundary of a four-dimensional figure, which cannot be a two-dimensional surface.

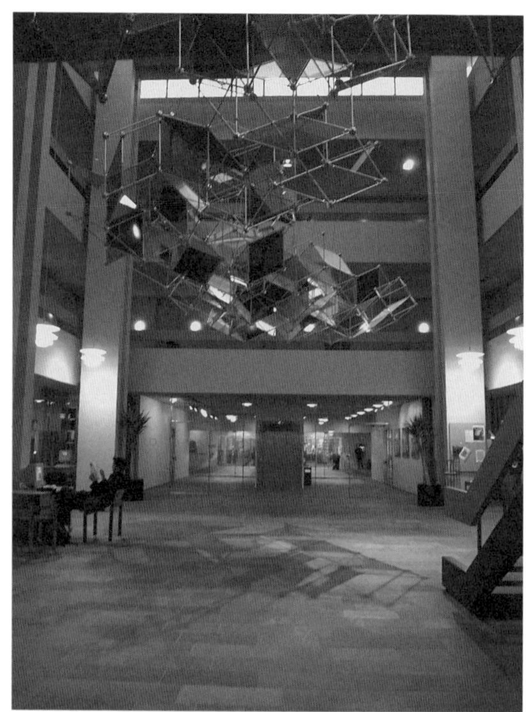

FIGURE 6 The Quasicrystal for Denmark's Technical University.
Aluminum bars and nodes with acrylic plates. 1989–94, destroyed in
2006. Approximately 17 meters in length. Photo: Annette Hartung

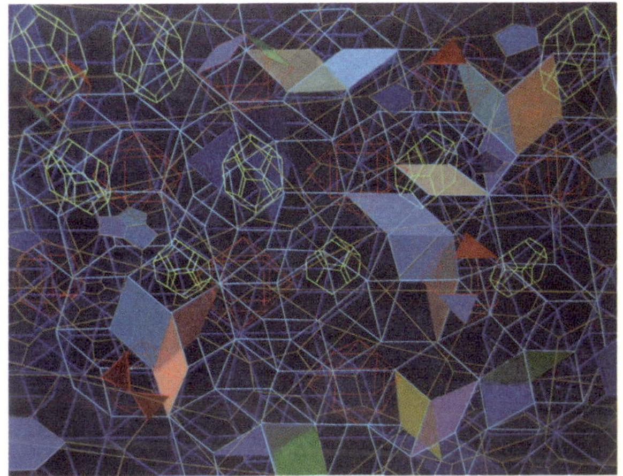

FIGURE 7 Painting numbered 07–6, Tony Robbin, 2007. Acrylic on canvass, 56 x 70 inches.

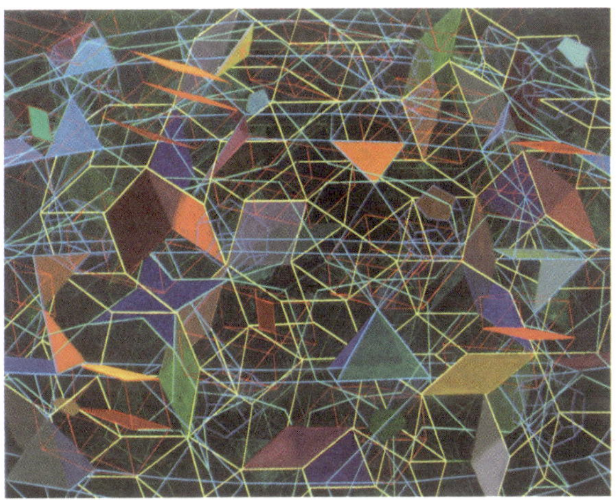

FIGURE 8 Painting numbered 06–1, Tony Robbin, 2006. Acrylic on canvass, 56 x 70 inches.

1. L Henderson, *The Fourth Dimension and Non-Euclidean Geometry in Modern Art,* Princeton University Press, Princeton, N J, 1983. For a fuller discussion of Picasso's use of four-dimensional geometry, see also T Robbin, *Shadows of Reality, The Fourth Dimension in Relativity, Cubism and Modern Thought,* New Haven and London, 2006.

2. J Palau i Fabre, *Picasso Cubism (1907–1917),* Rizzoli, New York, 1990.

3. L Henderson, 'Modernism and Science', in *Modernism,* V Liska and A. Eysteinsson (eds.), John Benjamins, Amsterdam, 2005.

To Martin, from Gheri.

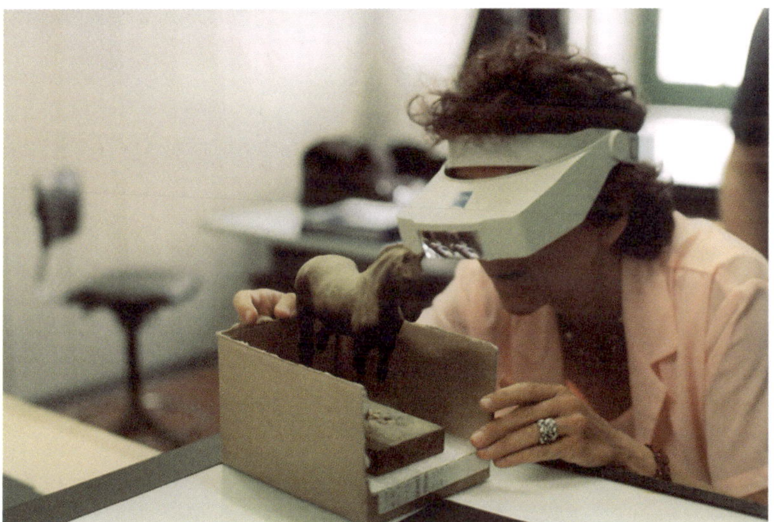

Acts of looking, Study for Monumento Sforza, wax model, Opificio delle Pietre Dure, Florence.

Part II – Images

Richard Wentworth

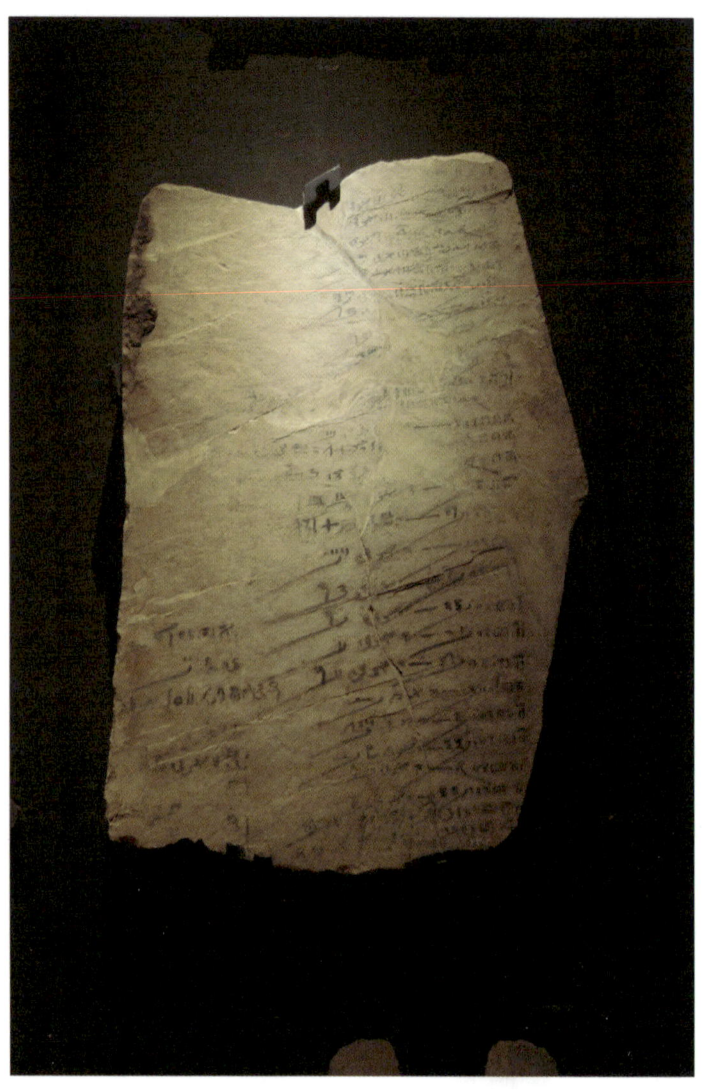

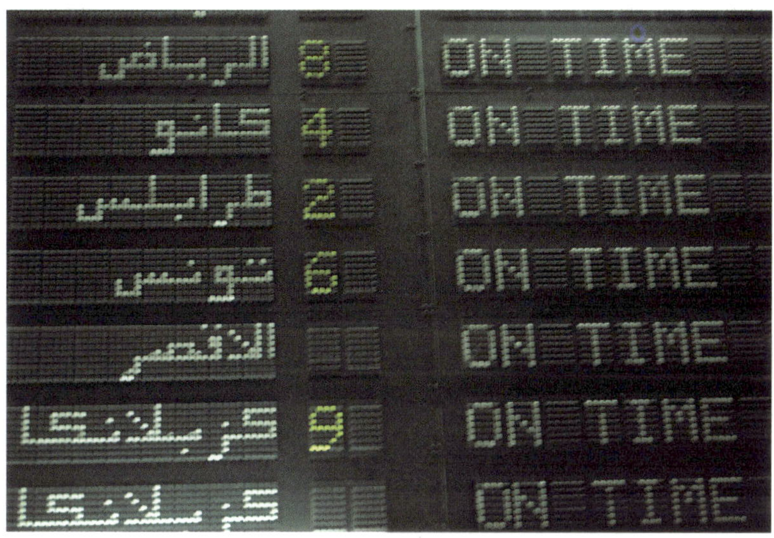

Dear Assimina and Marina,

I know we're a long way from the art directed finale, but I have an idea which I think can work as a two page spread. It's visual, very Ancient and very Modern, pictures taken on the same day, in Cairo, in a museum and at the airport. As is often the case they're not my greatest photographs, but they do have content. I think they will need some professional attention and we would have to discuss the finer points of layout. Here they are. One is an Ostrakon, the other, I suppose, would become an Ostrakon on the day they turn off the electric power. Obviously all this has to work on the page, and in context, so let me know where things are going.

Richard

Susan Derges

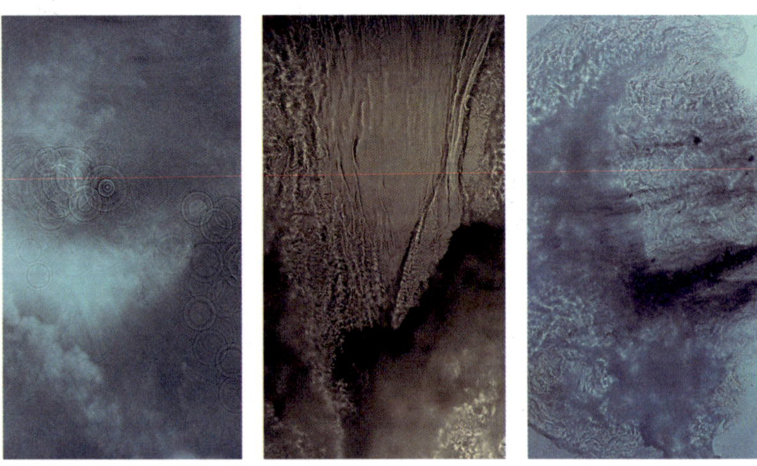

Reflections on liquid form: the music of waves, the poetry of particles. (Thoughts on implicate order for Susan Derges) by Martin Kemp 1999   Eddies, vortices, standing waves, cascades, fractals, give form to an event, a thought, an image – the observer and the observed are engaged in a dialogue, a process of feedback, of unbroken wholeness between entities of similar natures. Mental phenomena are resonating with dynamic external systems in states of continuously metamorphosing chaos and order. Even as apparently substantial forms and thoughts crystalise out of this complexity of interactions their demise is already unfolding – cloud becomes

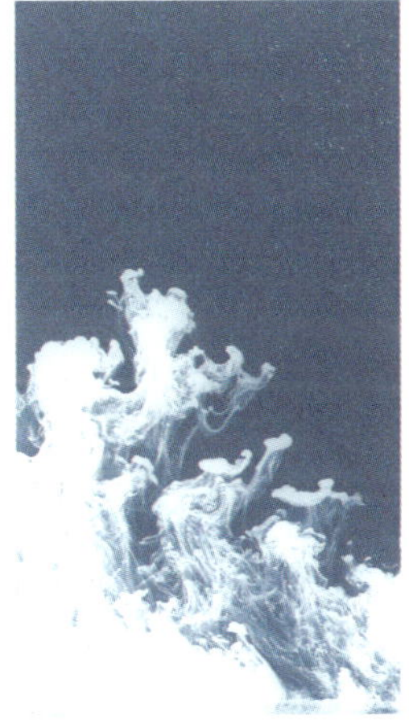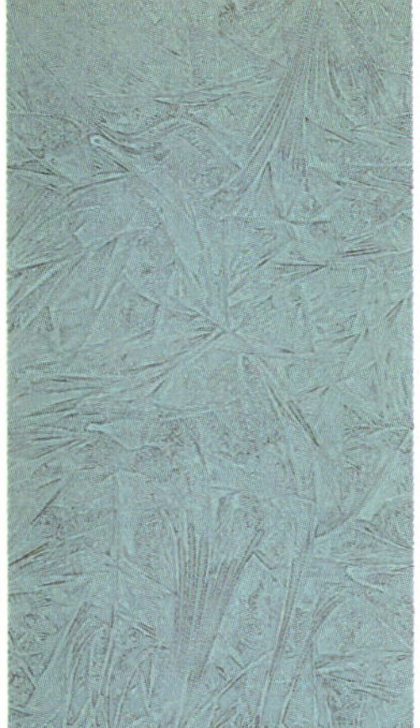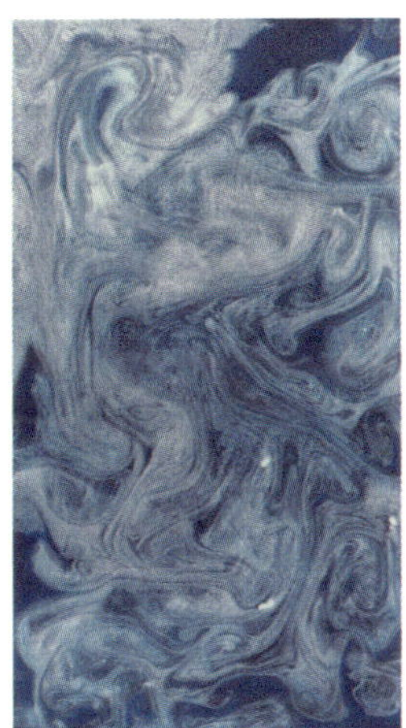

rainfall, thought forms dissipate, new ones emerge out of a complex web of stimuli. Rainfall becomes pool, stream becomes torrent river, ocean evaporates and distils as cloud. Unseen structures are imagined and found in the external world and visa versa as our perceiving consciousness interacts, processes and structures with the innate geometries and systems it is endowed with – that resonate with external patterns, recurring across scales, species and matter. Every perception is a co-creation – a structural intuition – of an underlying musical score.

Karl Grimes

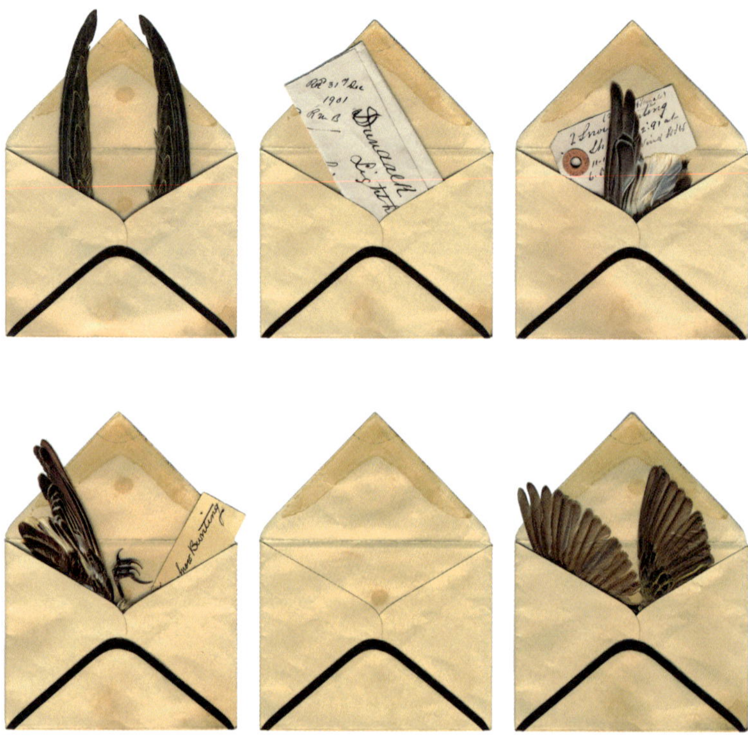

Karl Grimes. *Killed Striking*. 2007. Grid of 39 Archival pigment prints (detail), 122 x 366 cm. Archival canvas map and LED light work, 180 x 120 cm. Sound work 6.07 minutes (**Karl Grimes** & Tom Lawrence). Edition of 2. Collection of the artist and National Museum of Ireland.

Fatal light   Stacked high above specimen cabinets in a storage area of the Natural History Museum in Dublin are dozens of dusty black boxes arranged in ordered rows like cemetery stone tablets. Inside are hundreds of bird wings, feathers, claws, envelopes, invoices, letters and assorted bird body parts, all neatly grouped and labeled. Their contents, at once timeless yet utterly of their time and place, have remained largely untouched since they were bequeathed to the Museum in 1916. These are the archives and life's project of R M Barrington (1849–1915), naturalist, collector, innovatory quantifier and author of *The Migration of Birds as Observed at Irish Lighthouses and Lightships*, in 1900.   ¶   Barrington was obsessed with the migratory patterns of birds around the Irish coastline, still very much an inexact science in the late 19th century. His quest for hard evidence and fact, beyond random observation and untrained account, fuelled the remarkable project he began in 1881, a pioneering, systematic and idiosyncratic study that continued for over twenty years.   ¶   He secured the voluntary participation of Irish lightship and lighthouse keepers, marshalling them into a far-flung body of researchers and observers. Aware of the fatal attraction that birds have to artificial light, he directed his team to collect all avian victims found after daytime fog and nocturnal strikes with the lighthouse lantern beams. These were then placed in standard envelopes with schedules and comments for collection by the Irish Lights relief ships and delivery via Royal Mail to Barrington's home in County Wicklow. Over two decades, thousands of visitor and passage migrant birds of various species were labeled, classified, measured, preserved and quantified.   ¶   *Killed Striking* imagines Barrington's passion, his vast archive of birds, the lightkeepers' logs and comments, allied to the re-creation of a sequence of migratory flight paths – sightlines, scapes and lunar phases – directly preceding the points of impact. Using photography and sound in a process of inquiry and collaboration, the work re-interprets the Barrington archive at the National Museum of Ireland, re-thinking perspectives behind empirical science and conventions of display.

Karl Grimes *Killed Striking* is from the exhibition and artist's monograph *Dignified Kings Play Chess On Fine Green Silk*, with a forward by Martin Kemp. Published by the Gallery of Photography, Ireland and the National Museum of Ireland, 2007.

Tim O'Riley

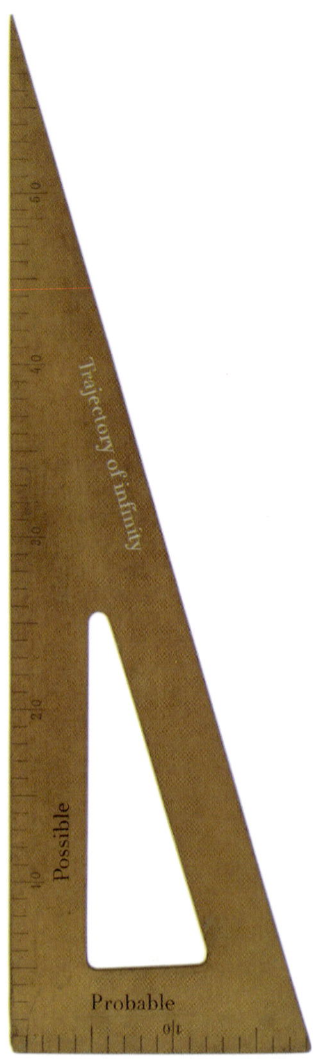

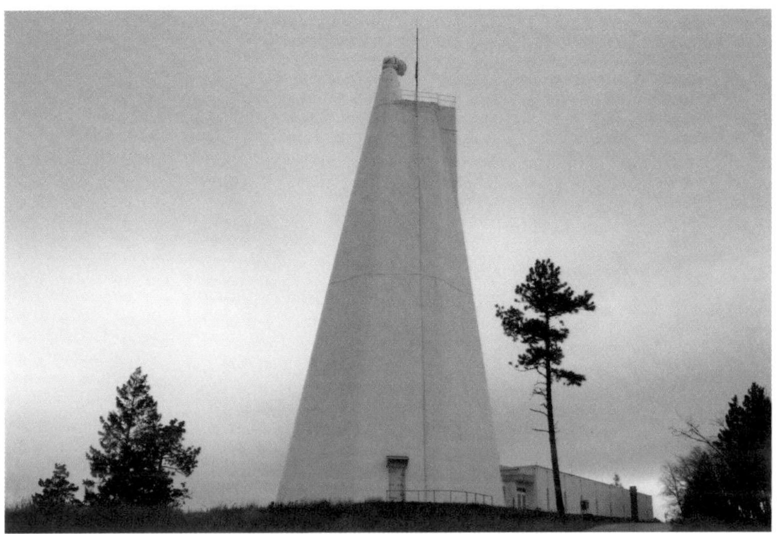

FIGURE 1 *Speculative Object*, 2008, sign paint, wooden set square, 60 x 20 x 0.4 cm.   FIGURE 2 *The Vacuum Tower*, 2006.

The world has been described, mapped and measured to such a degree that these measurements at times seem natural. These two works – both featuring mapping instruments of a kind – are for me synonymous with this thought, at once technically sophisticated but simple too. The photograph above was taken on a rainy day at the National Solar Observatory, high up on a mountain in New Mexico. It shows the Vacuum Tower, a telescope used to observe the sun. Over 100 metres from top to bottom, much of the instrument is housed underground. I found the set square, opposite, in a town near Mont Ventoux in southern France. Less familiar than the plastic, everyday tools I was used to, its form was suggestive of matters beyond utility. It was at once a device for surveying and measuring and yet curiously representative of something else, a prompt for thoughts of other spaces or dimensions. I had it inscribed – with the help of a sign writer – with words that seemed to chime with this sense or logic.

Cecil Balmond

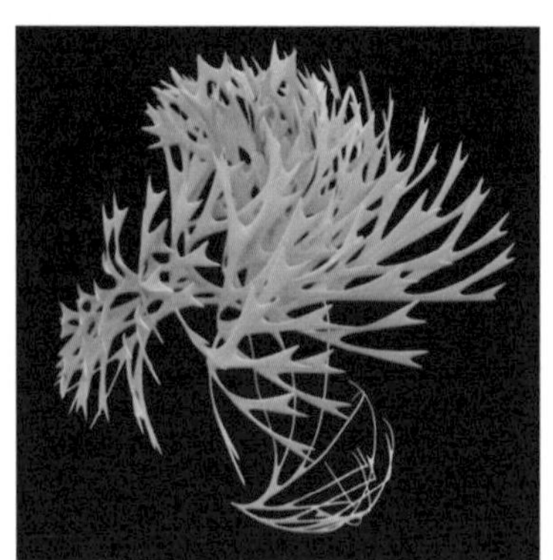 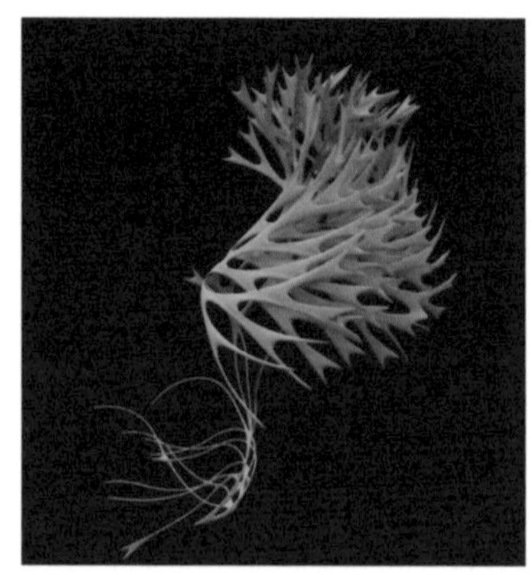

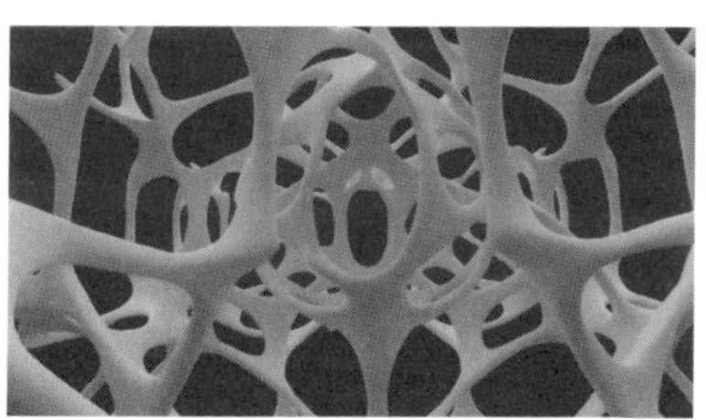 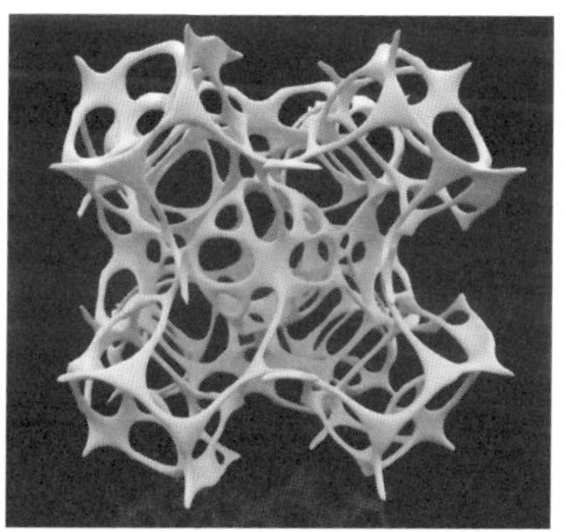

Organic looking forms derived from an abstract grid of numbers that has strict internal rigour. The order comes from four number series that have self reflecting properties and combine to form deep symmetries. The numbers seem to provide a fine grain in the data environment to produce crystalline or organic forms.

Kate Whiteford

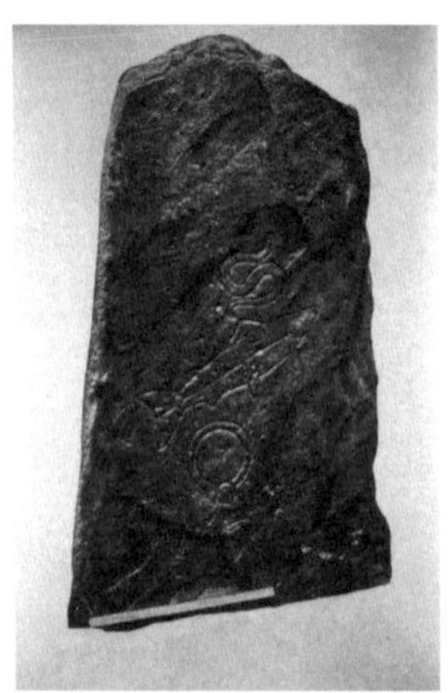

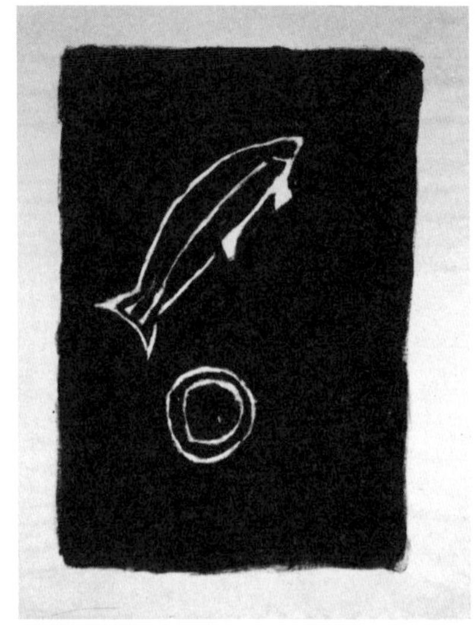

FIGURES 1–4 *Sculpure for Calton Hill*, Edinburgh, 1987.
(Opposite page, top) View from the top of the Nelson Monument, a tower in the shape of an upturned telescope. The act of seeing, of looking through the wrong end of a telescope, is intrinsic to the functioning of the work. The images were drawn anamorphically and appeared merely abstract at ground level. The images would reveal themselves after climbing the 143 steps of the Nelson Monument. Based on the incised stone at Gamis Manse, Angus (illustrated above), this work was the final piece in a series of work following a residency at St Andrews University. cf Kemp, Martin: *Sitelines. Kate Whiteford*, Graeme Murray, Edinburgh 1992.

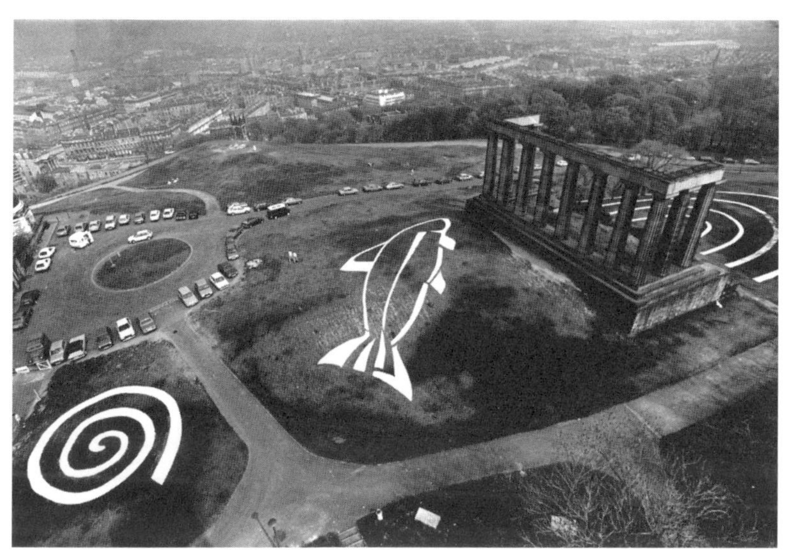

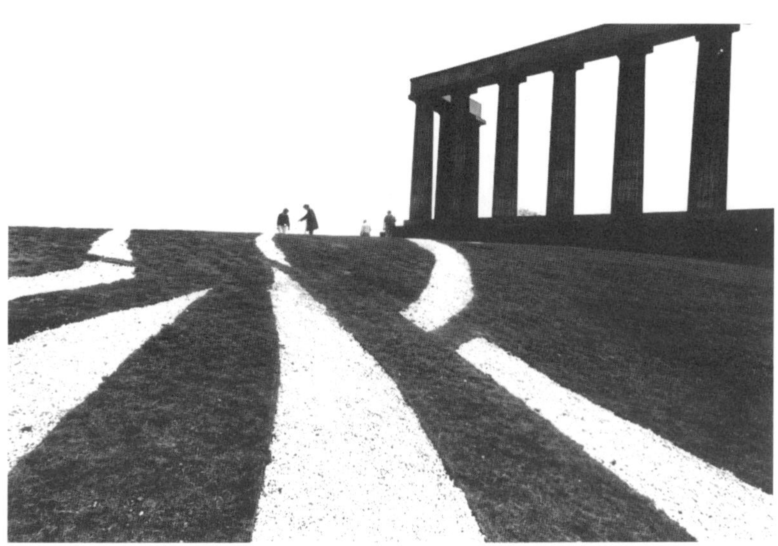

Paul Williams

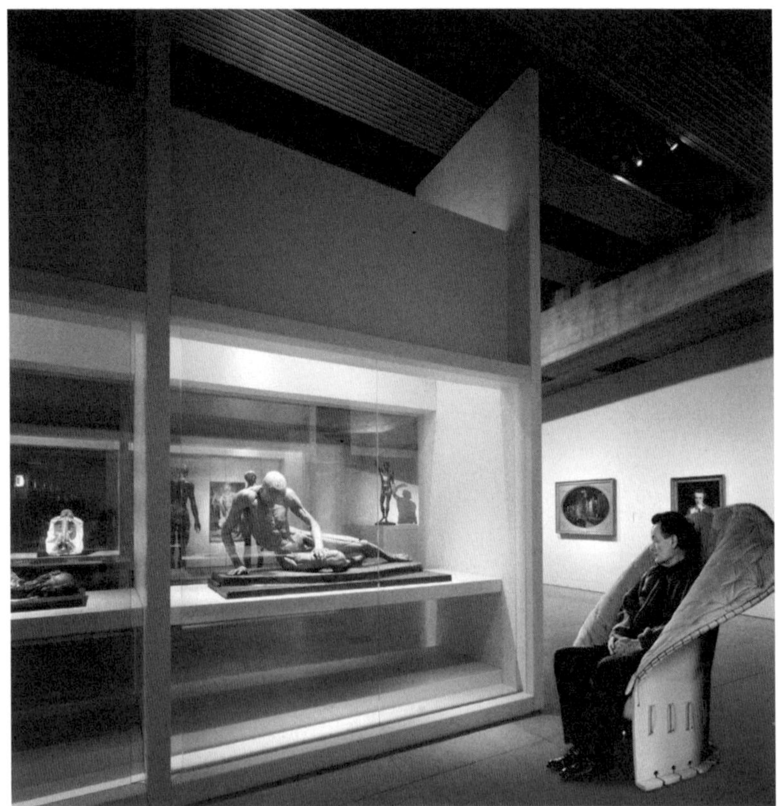

Spectacular Bodies Spectacular Mind

Katharine Dowson

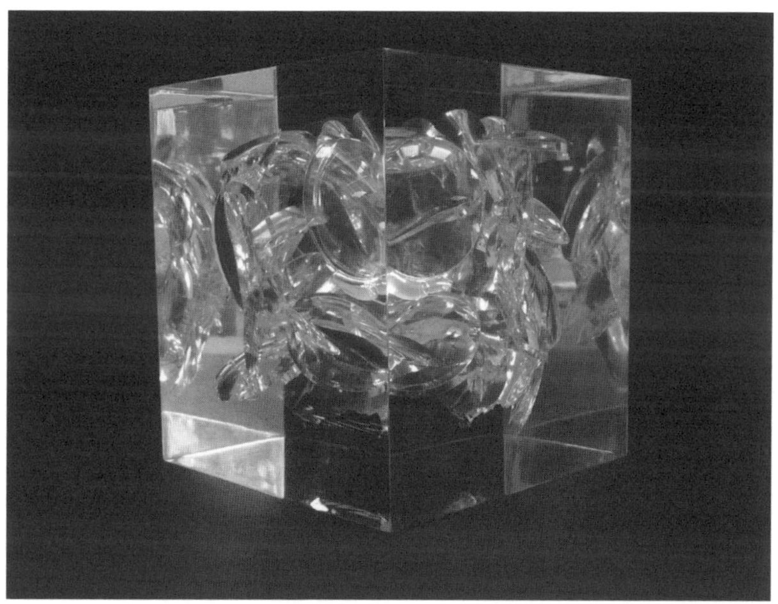

Micro Macro, 2009, acrylic, clear glass optical lenses, 19 x 17.5 x 17.5 cm.

Part III – Essays

Pietro C Marani

Vedere la storia del collezionismo in un disegno di Leonardo al Louvre: filologia e attribuzione

The history of collecting 'seen' in a Leonardo drawing at the Louvre: philology and attribution

Nella recente edizione dei disegni di Leonardo e della sua cerchia che si conservano nelle collezioni francesi,[1] ho ripreso, fra l'altro, in esame la storia collezionistica del fondo di disegni di Leonardo che si conserva attualmente nel Département des Arts Graphiques du Louvre, intrecciandola con un ripetuto esame degli originali. Molte sorprese ha riservato, in particolare, lo studio del gruppo di sei disegni eseguiti a pennello su tela di lino raffiguranti studi di panneggi che provengono dalla collezione seicentesca di Everhard Jabach e che sono stati considerati insieme ad altri tre disegni, due attualmente conservati nel Musée des Beaux Arts di Rennes e uno nella Fondation Custodia, Institut Néerlandais, Collection Frits Lugt a Parigi, di identica provenienza. Questi nove studi, a loro volta, fanno parte di un gruppo di quattordici tele, tutte identificate da Bernadette Py (2001) come provenienti dalla Collezione Jabach, cinque dei quali si trovano in altri Musei: uno nel Kupferstichkabinett di Berlino, due nel British Museum, e altri due nella raccolta Piasecka Johnson a Princeton (New Jersey). Altri disegni simili, attribuiti a Leonardo, ma di diversa provenienza, si trovano invece nel Gabinetto Disegni e delle Stampe della Galleria degli Uffizi a Firenze. Mi sembra questo omaggio alla figura di Martin Kemp, alla sua pervicace e infaticabile ricerca sui meccanismi della visione, l'occasione più opportuna per ricapitolare quelli che credo siano da considerare elementi di novità circa la distinzione delle parti autografe, dovute a Leonardo, in questo gruppo di disegni, e quelle invece aggiunte successivamente, e, allo stesso tempo, per farne un caso esemplare di studio circa il legame inscindibile che si è venuto a creare tra analisi visiva delle opere d'arte, filologia, attribuzione e storia dell'arte. ¶ Le quattordici tele di lino sono citate per la prima volta nell'inventario postumo del 1695 della collezione di Everhard Jabach (1618–1695) con l'attribuzione a Dürer: '14 Etudes de draperie d'Alber Dure (sic) sur toile collée sur papier et haussée de blanc en détrempe.'[2] Acquistate da Pierre Crozat, furono attribuite dal Mariette, nel catalogo della vendita della sua collezione del 1741, a Leonardo e raggruppate sotto al n. 5, che includeva però anche altri quattro disegni di teste. Venduti a Nourri, nella vendita della collezione di quest'ultimo, avvenuta nel 1785, dei quattordici iniziali non ne figurano che due (sotto al numero 736) attribuiti ancora a Dürer. Giorgio Vasari[3] ricordava però, nella *Vita* di Leonardo,[4] come l'artista 'studiò assai di ritrar di naturale, e qualche volta in far modelli di figure di terra; e addosso a quelle metteva cenci molli interrati, e poi con pazienza si metteva a ritrargli sopra certe tele sottilissime di rensa o di panni lini adoperati, e li lavorava di nero e bianco con la punta del pennello ch'era cosa miracolosa; come ancora ne fan fede alcuni che ho di sua mano in sul nostro libro de' disegni ...,' così che il riferimento a Leonardo degli studi a noi pervenuti si affacciò prepotentemente alla critica che si basò, oltre che sulle parole del Vasari, sulla qualità dei disegni nonché su alcune scritte antiche presenti sulle tele di lino: in particolare riferimenti a Leonardo in scrittura antica si trovano sulla tela del British Museum, inv. 1895–9–15–487, e su quella di Rennes, inv. 794–1–2506, mentre, i nomi 'Leonardo/Verrocchio' si trovano segnati modernamente al verso del disegno degli Uffizi 420 E. Un motivo di ulteriore affinità, e che accomuna molti disegni fra loro, è dato dalla presenza di numeri romani, segnati, solitamente in alto, da quella che sembra una stessa mano: il numero 'I' su Louvre 2256; il numero 'III' su Rennes, inv. 794–1–2507, e anche su Louvre, RF 1081; il numero 'IV' su Louvre, RF 41904; il numero 'V' su Rennes, inv. 794–1–2506; il numero 'IX' su Louvre RF 1082; il numero 'X' su quello ex de Ganay, oggi in coll. Piasecka Johnson e il numero 'XII' sull'altro della stessa collezione a Princeton; il numero 'XIII' su Louvre RF 41905 e, finalmente, anche su Fondation Custodia, coll. F Lugt, inv. 6632. Una prima osservazione da fare è che i fogli degli Uffizi non presentano questo tipo di numerazione, così da suggerire che essa sia da considerarsi non antichissima (e certo non originale, o del tempo di Leonardo) e apposta dopo una prima dispersione del gruppo o, cosa ancor più ipotetica, che possa essere stata apposta da qualcuno successivamente al Vasari (ritenendo che quelli degli Uffizi provengano, molto più probabilmente degli altri, dal suo *Libro*). La seconda è che la ripetizione di alcuni numeri romani (il numero 'III' compare due volte, e così il numero 'XIII') potrebbe indicare l'esistenza non di un'unica serie, originariamente unita, ma di almeno due, distinte già in antico o per eventuale diversità di mano o per storia collezionistica diversa. Nonostante ciò, Wickoff (1899) e Degenhart, introducevano per primi, rispettivamente, i nomi di Domenico Ghirlandajo e di Fra' Bartolommeo mentre per Berenson, nella seconda edizione dei *Florentine Drawings* (1938), le tele di lino si sarebbero dovute dividere tra Leonardo, il Sogliani e Tommaso. Jean Cadogan (1983) propose, più di recente, un'ulteriore nuova divisione di mani all'interno del gruppo: gli studi apparterrebbero parte al Ghirlandajo, parte al Verrocchio e parte a Leonardo, e questo fondandosi su riscontri con opere affrescate, scolpite o dipinte da questi artisti e su un esame del modo in cui problemi di rappresentazione degli effetti di luce sono affrontati nei diversi disegni. Il punto di vista della Cadogan veniva contestato da Gigetta Dalli Regoli (1985) che, giudicando non soddisfacenti le motivazioni addotte dalla Cadogan per assegnare il gruppo dei monocromi su lino a differenti artisti, sottolineava l'impostazione sperimentale degli studi 'che non potevano essere analizzati e qualificati esclusivamente in relazione con opere di scultura e di pittura.'[5] La Viatte, poco dopo (1989), ribadendo l'unitarietà della serie (che comprende, secondo la studiosa, sedici e non diciassette pezzi: esclude il foglio del British Museum 1895–1–15–487), di cui sottolinea le somiglianze tecniche ed esecutive (ma anche qualche differenza) e il riferimento a Leonardo, ribadiva che le tele, 'sans finalité immediate,' 'traditionnelles et novatrices, impersonnelles et magistrales … bien accordées à ses propres écrits, ne doivent pas, semble-t-il, étre attribuées à un autre artiste que lui-meme.'[6] Ma, nuovamente, Keith Christiansen riapriva (1990) il problema dell'appartenenza della serie a quel genere di lavoro collettivo che si sa essere stata la caratteristica, attorno al 1470, della bottega del Verrocchio, individuando, all'interno del gruppo, autografi di Leonardo ma anche, appunto, del Verrocchio. Io stesso avevo parzialmente aderito a questo tipo di lettura[7] individuando, ad esempio nella tela degli Uffizi 433 E, uno studio del Verrocchio per la figura di Cristo nel gruppo dell'*Incredulità di Tommaso*, rapportando lo studio alle fasi di progettazione e di fusione del gruppo, così come altri studiosi[8] avevano continuato ad individuare in certi fogli la mano del Ghirlandajo. Così la Cadogan che, nella sua monografia sul Ghirlandajo (2000), riconfermava a quest'artista il celebre panneggio nel disegno del Louvre 2255. L'omogeneità dell'intera serie, per tecnica esecutiva, tipo di supporto, e, per almeno quattordici di essa, per la stessa provenienza seicentesca, cioè dalla collezione Jabach, è stata ritenuta dalla Viatte elemento di un certo peso, e altamente significativo, anche per l'attribuzione del gruppo alla stessa mano, e cioè a Leonardo da Vinci.[9] La studiosa riesaminava di nuovo l'intero problema, ribadendo le sue convinzioni sull'omogeneità della serie e l'autografia leonardesca, ma accogliendo, in parte, quelle che erano state le prime risultanze del nuovo attento esame da me condotto (maggio 2001) sullo stato di conservazione delle tele. La serie deve essere nata all'interno della bottega del Verrocchio come esercizio di studio e di addestramento del giovane Leonardo, aperta però, almeno inizialmente, ad interventi del Verrocchio o di qualche altro artista. Ne consegue che, ad esempio, per i disegni di Rennes (o per il 433 E degli Uffizi e il disegno di Berlino inv. 5039), ci si possa ancora interrogare sulla possibilità di una condivisione di mano o di esecuzione da parte del Verrocchio. Su questa linea sono anche il Nathan,[10] che reintroduce per il disegno di Rennes 794–1–2506 il riferimento a Fra' Bartolommeo, e per l'altro a Rennes 794–1–2507 la formula dubitativa 'Leonardo o Verrocchio?' (riferendo il disegno di Berlino inv. 5039 a 'Leonardo o Domenico Ghirlandajo?'), e Carmen C Bambach che, in un contributo (2004), che seguiva le due mostre di Parigi e di New York del 2003, proponeva infatti anch'essa di negare la paternità di Leonardo per i due disegni di Rennes, attribuendo il 794–1–2507 al Verrocchio e il 794–1–2506 a un maestro anonimo.   ¶   Ma elementi nuovi sono emersi considerando la possibilità che alcuni di questi disegni siano stati, durante il Seicento, 'ritoccati' o 'abbelliti' o, ancora, restaurati e integrati, dagli artisti che lavoravano per Jabach, nel tentativo di rendere più 'finiti,' quelli che potevano apparire, al gusto dell'epoca, disegni semplicemente 'abbozzati' e, soprattutto, in previsione di una vendita della raccolta, o di una parte di essa, al Re di Francia, come era infatti avvenuto per 'schizzi' di Annibale Carracci e di altri artisti antichi. L'eventualità che su alcune di queste tele si potessero rintracciare e definire interventi d'altra mano, rendeva infatti ragione delle oscillazioni attributive avanzate dalla critica. Gli studi pioneristici di Catherine Monbeig Goguel (1986) sui disegni di provenienza Jabach venduti al re di Francia, hanno messo in luce ritocchi e integrazioni seicentesche sui disegni dei maestri antichi presenti nella sua raccolta, per la maggior parte dovuti a Michelle Corneille. Così, i disegni su tela di lino attribuiti prima a Duerer e, poi, a Leonardo, esaminati sotto a questa luce, giustificavano i pareri diversi sulla qualità e la finalità degli studi stessi, in quanto resi disomogenei da interventi (e da uno stato di conservazione di volta in volta diverso) successivi e di completamento (rifacimenti con bianco coprente, rinforzi nei rialzi di biacca, allargamenti dei panneggi o campiture piatte d'ombra con grezze pennellate di bistro, gli accenni a busti, braccia e teste, ad esempio, che non sembravano del tutto autorizzare il riferimento a Leonardo per la loro corsività, lo stile e la mancanza di riscontri con l'opera grafica di Leonardo nell'ottavo decennio del Quattrocento). Uno studio di panneggio come quello al Louvre, inv. 2255, esaminato attentamente, può fornire indicazioni preziose circa il sovrapporsi di interventi e porsi come un esempio significativo dei rapporti tra filologia e attribuzione. ¶ Questo studio è infatti stato riferito anticamente[11] anche a Lorenzo di Credi (una cui copia tratta da questo disegno si trova nel British Museum di Londra, n. 1895–9–15–459, mentre uno studio simile sempre del Credi è nell'Institut Néerlandais di Parigi, n. 2491, entrambi assai diversi per stile e tecnica, essendo di conduzione più morbida, con una minore accentuazione dei chiaroscuri, ed essendo disegnati su carta preparata rossa o rosa), Verrocchio e Domenico Ghirlandajo. Carlo Pedretti, per parte sua, ha invece ripetutamente confermato l'attribuzione a Leonardo di questo disegno e ha anche accostato a questo del Louvre un piccolo studio di panneggio di Leonardo in penna e inchiostro conservato nel Codice Atlantico, f. 1021 recto (ex 366 recto–a), e databile verso il 1495–97[12] (benché questo accostamento non sia probante ai fini dell'attribuzione della tela del Louvre n. 2255 a Leonardo ed essendo i due studi separati fra loro da più di vent'anni, per di più essendo di tecnica, destinazione e scopo assai diversi), e così ha fatto di recente Jacques Franck.[13] Ma l'attribuzione al Ghirlandajo si è riaffacciata ripetutamente anche in tempi molto recenti (Fahy, Cadogan, Nathan dubitativamente) e si regge sul confronto tipologico con il panneggio della Vergine che compare nella pala di San Giusto del Ghirlandajo ora negli Uffizi a Firenze (*Madonna in trono con i santi Michele, Giusto, Zanobi e Raffaele*, tavola, cm. 200 x 191), confronto per la prima volta proposto dal Woefflin (1899) e quindi considerato dal Wickoff (1899) come la prova della paternità ghirlandajesca del disegno del Louvre. Ma, oltre che ricordare, come hanno fatto di recente la Dalli Regoli[14] e la Viatte,[15] la pericolosità di confrontare questi studi con dipinti, spesso tra loro distanti cronologicamente,[16] c'è da osservare che il disegno sottostante il panneggio nel dipinto del Ghirlandajo, messo in luce dalle riflettografie all'infrarosso recentemente effettuate, ha mostrato un *ductus* e una conduzione molto diversi da quanto emerge ad un attento esame del monocromo su lino del Louvre,[17] oltretutto di dimensioni, certo ragguardevoli, ma che difficilmente può, a rigore, essere considerato uno studio specifico (non certo un 'cartone') per la ben più grande composizione del Ghirlandajo, ragion per cui la Bambach,[18] oltre che la Viatte e gran parte della critica più recente (incluso Christiansen), ha ribadito con forza l'attribuzione dello studio a Leonardo.   ¶   L'esecuzione finissima in punta di pennello di questo studio,[19] ne fa il migliore di tutta la serie, di cui il disegno costituisce un punto d'arrivo ineguagliato. Ciononostante, l'esame ripetuto fatto dallo scrivente su questo monocromo in occasione della preparazione della Mostra del Louvre del 2003, con l'assistenza di Françoise Viatte e di Varena Forcione,[20] ha portato ad osservare l'esistenza di svariati ritocchi e di qualche ripassatura di epoca successiva. In particolare ritocchi in grigio più scuro si notano nell'angolo inferiore sinistro e destro, come per nascondere una piccola macchia o un timbro. Pennellate leggermente più pastose di bianco si osservano nelle pieghe in basso a sinistra e sul ginocchio in alto a sinistra (ginocchio destro della figura). La campitura in grigio chiaro in alto a destra sembra anch'essa un rifacimento, dato che essa appare coprente, mentre subito al di sotto la stesura originale appare abrasa. Così il primo piano, su cui una leggera ripassatura coprente contrasta con lo stato generale della stesura rimanente, dove si osservano invece abrasioni generalizzate e minute. Inoltre, il forte plasticismo dello studio potrebbe essere stato accentuato anche da una ripassatura delle zone d'ombra. E' singolare e stupefacente che molti finissimi tratti realizzati in punta di pennello e di colore quasi nero, come nell'ombra laterale della gamba sinistra, o nella lunga cavità ombrosa fra le pieghe del panneggio in corrispondenza di questa gamba (a destra di chi guarda), fin quasi a terra, presentino un andamento dall'alto a destra verso il basso a sinistra, come se fossero stati tracciati con la mano destra. Vero è che, nella parte di sinistra del disegno, a lato delle pieghe centrali più illuminate, fra le gambe, o, ancora, sotto le pieghe illuminate che coprono il ginocchio sinistro, nella zona d'ombra subito sotto ad esso, in alto a destra sulla tela, gli stessi tratti presentano andamento opposto, dall'alto a sinistra verso il basso a destra, sembrando disegnati con la mano sinistra. Si pone dunque il problema o dell'esecuzione dello studio da parte di un artista che lavora con la mano destra (cioè: da parte di un artista diverso da Leonardo), o dell'intervento di un altro pittore (in epoca successiva, e diverso da Leonardo), o, infine, se si ammette che tutti questi tratteggi, risultando identici per *ductus*, siano di Leonardo, del capovolgimento, da parte sua, della tela in fase esecutiva via via che si rendeva necessario seguire l'andamento obliquo delle pieghe e definire le loro ombre, assecondandone le diagonali da destra verso sinistra o viceversa. E' comunque strano che anche i più pastosi rialzi di bianco sembrino anch'essi condotti con la mano destra. Si dovrebbe dunque pensare all'intervento di un abilissimo ritoccatore che ha assecondato molto bene il gioco di luci ed ombre suggerito dalle pieghe dei panni intervenendo con ripassature e rinforzi di bianco che, tuttavia, non sembra coincidere con la mano di Michelle Corneille e che potrebbe, in linea d'ipotesi, essere anche un artista più antico. L'effetto di forte plasticità e la finezza di questi interventi indurrebbero a ripensare ai percorsi più antichi del disegno e a valutare se figure di raccoglitori o collezionisti come Francesco Melzi o Pompeo Leoni non possano aver contribuito a preservare le invenzioni e i disegni di Leonardo cercando di mantenerli sempre ben leggibili ed, eventualmente, anche a ritoccarli via via nel tempo.   ¶   Certo, questo studio e gli altri della serie, confermano una visione delle cose, della luce e delle ombre, del modo, infine, di risolvere per forza di 'lumi' il rilievo, che non può essere che di Leonardo, pur tenendo a mente come, ad un esame dettagliato, molti dei tratteggi sembrino condotti con la mano destra. Proprio a questo riguardo si può infine osservare come anche la labile traccia di tratteggi sui panni in corrispondenza della gamba destra (a sinistra per chi guarda) servita per una prima impostazione del chiaroscuro, sembri rivelare un andamento dei tratteggi destrorso, ma quasi 'following the form,' come a prefigurare una tecnica disegnativa che Leonardo avrebbe adottato solo nell'ultimo decennio del Quattrocento.

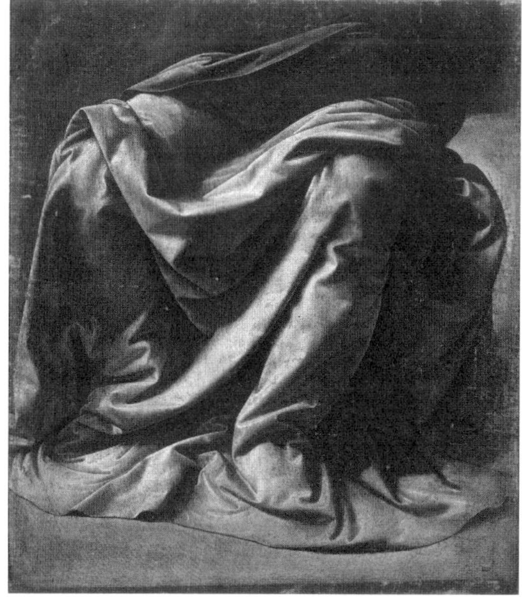

FIGURE 1 Leonardo da Vinci, *Drapery for a Seated Figure,* 1470
© R M N.

1. Vedi Pietro C Marani, *Disegni di Leonardo da Vinci e della sua cerchia nelle Collezioni pubbliche in Francia*, Edizione Nazionale dei Manoscritti e dei Disegni di Leonardo da Vinci, Firenze, Giunti Editore, 2008, cui si rimanda per tutta la bibliografia citata qui in forma abbreviata.

2. Bernadetty Py, *Everhard Jabach Collectionneur (1618–1695). Les dessins de l'inventaire de 1695*, Parigi, 2001. p.270.

3. Vedi Dalli Regoli, in Pedretti-Dalli Regoli 1985, pp.17–19, e 49–53, nn. 2–4, con bibl. precedente.

4. Vasari, ed. Bettarini-Barocchi 1976, p.17.

5. In Pedretti-Dalli Regoli 1985, p.50.

6. Viatte, in *Parigi* 1989, pp.21 e 32.

7. Pietro Cesare Marani, in *Leonardo da Vinci, una carriera di pittore*, Milano-Arles, 1999.

8. Ad es. Schulze Altencapperberg 1996.

9. Viatte, in *New York* 2003, pp.111–120, e in *Parigi, Louvre*, 2003/1, pp.53–59.

10. In Zoellner 2003.

11. Oltre che, come gli altri della serie, a Duerer: su cui vedi le penetranti osservazioni di Chastel, in *Parigi* 1989, pp.11–14h.

12. cfr. Pedretti, *The Codex Atlanticus ... Part Two*, 1979, p.238.

13. In Galluzzi 2006.

14. 1985, p.50.

15. In *New York* e in *Parigi* 2003.

16. La Pala di San Giusto data, secondo la Cadogan, 2000, attorno al 1479–80, mentre Ronald G Kecks 1998, pp.117–118, pensa addirittura ad un'opera successiva al 1480, e che si sa essere stata sistemata sull'altare già entro il 1486: entrambe le cronologie mal s'adattano a questo studio di panneggio di Leonardo.

17. Vedi Bambach 2004, fig.14 a p.54.

18. Ivi, p.45 e passim.

19. Ma per un forte ingrandimento della parte centrale vedi in Zoellner 2003, pp.360–61; l'ingrandimento è straordinario perché consente di apprezzare tutti i tratti in punta di pennello, soprattutto nelle parti in ombra dei panneggi.

20. Di cui ha dato qualche anticipazione la stessa Viatte, nei cataloghi delle esposizioni di Parigi, p.70, e di New York, p.290, dello stesso 2003.

Katerina Reed-Tsocha

Having an eye for the problem

In 'Approaches to the History of Art,' an essay reflecting on questions of method and their application in art history, Ernst Gombrich recalls a seminar in which 'Cupology' was invented. 'Cupology' takes as its object a common teacup and encompasses all the questions this can possibly give rise to (questions of manufacture and provenance, social contexts, geographic origins, scientific facts relating to design, function, or even its contents), drawing upon all the disciplinary discourses that may be enlisted to answer them. 'If you asked why it had a handle, you needed some elementary physics to explain the conduction of heat to your fingers. You needed medicine to explain the popularity of tea as refreshment ...,' and then botany, geography, aesthetics, sociology, and so on. There is something remarkably holistic about this open-ended and ever-expanding model of interrelated discourses may at first seem to hover above an object. But Gombrich's point is that they do not just hover; for it is the object, closely observed, that defines their areas of intersection or overlap. The main difficulty is to resist the temptation to expand in all directions, to avoid going off in a tangent or yielding to 'the centrifugal tendencies of certain intellectual fashions;'[1] and the mechanism against these slips of art-historical judgement is a deceptively simple one: what holds it together is that it does not lose sight of the proverbial teacup. The approach (to use an extremely malleable term) differs from applying a pre-defined methodological framework, which is likely to overdetermine its interpretative outcome. Predictably, the theoretical toolkit offered to any student of art history today in the context of a 'core course in methodology,' like a set of fancy screwdrivers, does not impress Gombrich. His advice to the historian is to apply good judgement and common sense in knowing when he has gone over the top:

There are so many competing overriding theories offered to [the historian] – Marxism,

racialism, psychoanalysis, and any other global theory claiming to explain the whole

To which questions should be asked, this is all that Gombrich will disclose: 'What the historian needs in such matters,' he says, 'is some tact and some flair, what is called *having an eye for the problem*.'[3] ¶ It is an elegant and frustrating answer. 'Having an eye for the problem' may sound like the self-assured verdict of a gentleman scholar – a principle akin to Berensonian attributions – but it is most certainly not intended as such (and Gombrich has some things to say about Berenson's 'easy chatter' in this same essay). Instead, this ingeniously elliptical formula serves as a reminder that good standards are internal to scholarship (or in other words, for Gombrich is willing to give away only this much, we are guided by the tradition of research and the identification of a possibility to find out something new); and further, that particularity should not be sacrificed to generality, nor specificity to some general principle. And what about the multiplicity of discourses? Does this line of enquiry amount to transcending disciplinary boundaries? The answer for Gombrich is emphatically 'no,' for this would presuppose their validity: 'We are often exhorted to engage in interdisciplinary research, but I am far from sure that this is a valid issue. What we call disciplines are, at best, matters of organisational convenience in academic life.'[4] This sounds sensible but can be treacherous ground. For despite its initial user-friendly appearance, 'Cupology' seems to presuppose a great deal of well-internalised and sophisticated know-how but no easy prescription at the methodological level. ¶ In his own tribute to Gombrich,[5] Martin Kemp takes off from a remark made in this same paper, namely that we do not yet have an 'art history worthy of its name' because little attention is given to artistic achievement seen in terms of technical progress. Kemp's response – a detailed study of manifestations of graphic skill in Renaissance and Baroque engravings – is, appropriately for the occasion, an art-historical tour de force. Gombrich's influence is evident in Kemp's own approach to art history – ranging from direct references to key notions, such as 'matching and making' or 'schemata,' to much broader patterns – as is the affinity of ideas. Kemp has a deep distrust for the application of readymade methodological frameworks and, to put it euphemistically, an ideologically-entrenched lack of curiosity to find out what the method will deliver. (Here the temptation to resort to the anecdotal is great: many still remember the volcanic eruption that followed some, admittedly half-baked, reference to semiotics at a departmental seminar on photography some years ago. An amused peacemaker who tried to intervene whispering 'you are fierce' got the famous reply, loud and clear: 'I am right!') I suspect that if pushed to formulate a general methodological principle, Martin Kemp would not object greatly to resorting to Gombrich's formula of having an eye for the problem. This he certainly has. And it becomes even more evident (as well as necessary) when he sidesteps traditional disciplinary boundaries and expectations in his scholarly activity as a 'historian of the visual.' What are the affinities, if any, between his particular conception of visual studies – a term that has been used on a number of occasions in relation to the project, leading originally to the establishment of the Centre for Visual Studies at Oxford – and Gombrich's cupology?　¶　To continue the seminar theme, a paper Martin Kemp gave in the spring of 2005 at an interdisciplinary seminar series in Art History and Philosophy I used to organise at Trinity College came under the heading 'Not Art History and not Aesthetics.' The seminar proved, once again, memorable for reasons that would take us too far afield, but more relevantly it was the choice of title that seemed capable of igniting persistent disagreement. What the somewhat superfluous controversy that arose missed entirely, however, was that the paratactic negations alluded to the scholarly model endorsed by Kemp, the 'history of the visual.' This 'broad history of visual things'[6] is not a free-floating entity. It retains intricate links to art history, and, as I will argue, even involves unacknowledged premises that seem to lead directly to aesthetics. Arguably, this choice of terminology reflects to a certain extent a desire to distinguish the activity of 'the historian of the visual' from the now established field of 'visual studies.'　¶　Locating the differences depends on the exact usage of the terms 'visual studies' and 'visual culture', both of which allow a great deal of latitude.[7] Generally speaking, one of the key ideas underlying these new directions of thought is that the history of art is now superseded by a history of images, while one of the implications of this broader approach is the erosion of the traditional distinction between high and low art. The political overtones of this move should be obvious. 'For visual culture, visibility is not so simple,' writes Nicholas Mirzoeff. 'Its object of study is precisely the entities that come into being at the points of intersection of visibility with social power.'[8] According to this line of thinking, visual culture as a field is defined *by the questions it asks rather than the objects it studies,* questions concerning the constitution of the visual subject, politics of visual identity and related narratives leading to the construction of history. W J T Mitchell lists what fits into the domain of visual studies: scientific and technical imaging, film, television, digital media, philosophical inquiries into the epistemology of vision, semiotic studies of images and visual signs, psychoanalytic investigation of the scopic drive, phenomenological, physiological and cognitive studies of the visual process, sociological studies of spectatorship and display, visual anthropology, physics, optics and animal vision.[9] ¶ One parameter that defines the domain of visual studies is the prominence of theory. For example, in the volume *Visual Culture: Images and Interpretations,* edited by Norman Bryson, Michael Ann Holly and Keith Moxey (the same editorial team as for the earlier *Visual Theory: Painting and Interpretation*) the methodological approach is defined precisely in terms of theory. In the older volume, 'theory' enters the picture under the disguises of a variety of approaches that include phenomenology, analytic philosophy, as well as feminism and semiology; in the later one, the key player is poststructuralism. 'We simply wanted to see,' the editors explain, 'what would happen to the conception of the discipline as a discipline if theoretical issues were brought to the fore.'[10] The shift away from traditional disciplinary protocols involves a denaturalisation of aesthetics, that is, the rejection of the Kantian notion of aesthetic value, which is taken to be intrinsic to the work, and its replacement with a revised conception of aesthetic value arising from cultural conditions, and, closely related, an explicit focus on the cultural significance and historical circumstances of the production of the works (images). The model is one of methodological cross-fertilisation between art history and other disciplines in the humanities, while the central idea is that of the work of art redefined as a semiotic representation. ¶ Although by no means anti-theoretical, these are not the strands of theory that motivate Martin Kemp's approach. He describes the boundaries he aims to cross as those between territories of specialised knowledge,[11] and the aspirations of the historian of the visual in terms of extending modes of analysis normally reserved for works of art into the visual cultures of science and technology. The fact that this mode of analysis is not restricted to images implies points of intersection with yet another domain, that of cultural history.[12] The ambition is to establish the history of the visual as a distinctive discipline, as the following statement from the introduction to *Seen | Unseen* explains in detail: 'I am intending to explore the possibility of looking at issues in the public and professional debates in ways that at least raise interesting questions. Inevitably, [this] will be characterised as being about "art and science," an area of cross-disciplinary debate that become something of a growth industry. However, I wish it not to be seen as "art and science" but rather about "the history of the visual," *as a discipline in its own right*. I am operating on the assumption that if we do not begin by classifying each visual product as either a work of art or as a scientific product, some very interesting things begin to happen.'[13] The scope – as the approximately 300 pages of rich and suggestive connections that follow testify – is broad, and the approach is certainly distinctive, although too idiosyncratic to grow into an entire discipline. And it is the very same device that lends methodological rigour to the proposed model of the history of the visual (in sharp contrast to the fashionable sloppiness that plagues numerous other 'art-sci' attempts) that ultimately makes it idiosyncratic. The cornerstone is the notion of 'structural intuitions,' the structures of inner intuitive processes that are shared by artists and scientists, leading to the articulation of 'acts of seeing.' As is the case with all notions that have a major explanatory role to play, structural intuitions need to be defined with precision. Acts of seeing (of realities outside us), Kemp argues, are structured in terms of 'existing deposits of perceptual experience, pre-established criteria of interpretation, new and old acts of naming and classification, the physical parameters of our sensory apparatus and above all (and underlying all) deep structures operating at a pre- or sub- verbal level.' And continues with a strong claim: 'I subscribe to the view that the general potentialities and parameters of those deep structures (*ie* their rules of engagement with experience) are genetically established, while the precise manner in which they are realised, in terms of the laying down of 'hard-wiring' is shared by sensory and other experiences.'[14] There is plenty within this tantalisingly compressed assertion that still needs to be discussed and analysed in Kemp's work. More relevantly from my perspective, however, the introduction to *Visualisations: The nature book of art and science,* includes some intriguing observations that seem to indicate that the declaration 'not aesthetics' is not an entirely straightforward one.   ¶   So what about aesthetics? And even – to go back to that memorable seminar – what about pleasure? *Visualizations* begins with a 'double reading' of structural intuitions – which, rather surprisingly, comes across as a revised version of transcendental idealism. For, as Kemp argues, the structures are 'both those of the inner intuitive processes themselves and those of the external features whose structures are being intuited.'[15] From here it is only a short leap to aesthetics. This takes place soon enough when the question of aesthetic pleasure enters the picture. It can be claimed that in arguing that 'the aesthetic impulse is part of the feedback mechanism that reinforces our hugely demanding attempts to make coherent sense of those natural orders with which we can and must work if we are to survive,' and doing so in particular within a broader discussion of visual understanding, as well as by referring to our pleasure in pattern, symmetry and order, the discussion comes extremely close to Kantian aesthetics. In all fairness, Kemp's starting point is a discussion of the functionality and adaptation of our perceptual mechanism rather than transcendental idealism, and both nature and nurture are taken into account. And yet, at a more abstract level, one wonders whether what we see described in operation here is what Michael Podro calls the 'ordering mind.'[16] Accordingly, aesthetic judgement should be understood in terms of the activity of the mind that imposes structures on the world and in turn derives aesthetic delight from, precisely, the pattern, symmetry and order that it encounters in the world. Expanding this point further would require a lengthy analysis that falls beyond the scope of this short essay, and hence it must remain at the level of suggestion rather than sustained argument. Nevertheless, such an understanding could constitute an instance of what Martin Kemp describes as deeper realms of enquiry, going deeper in explaining, in philosophical terms, in what sense the aesthetic can be regarded as a shared instinct across the arts and sciences, and delivering a more nuanced notion of aesthetic pleasure.[17]

1. E H Gombrich, 'Approaches to the History of Art', in *Topics of our Time*, Phaidon, London, 1991, p.68.

2. Gombrich, p.66.

3. Gombrich, p.67.

4. Gombrich, p.67.

5. M Kemp 'Coming into line: Graphic demonstrations of skill in Renaissance and Baroque engravings' in *Sight and Insight: Essays on art and culture in honour of E H Gombrich at 85*, J Onians (ed.), Phaidon, London, 1994.

6. *Seen/Unseen: Art, Science and Intuition from Leonardo to the Hubble Telescope*, Oxford and New York, Oxford University Press, 2006. Cf. also 'Introduction' in M Kemp (ed.) *The Oxford History of Western Art*, Oxford University Press, Oxford and New York, 2000.

7. *Art History, Aesthetics and Visual Studies*, M A Holly and K Moxey (eds.), Williamstown, Mass., Clark Art Institute 2002. See J Elkins, *Visual Studies: A Skeptical Introduction*, Routledge, London and New York, 2003.

8. 'Ghostwriting: Working out Visual Culture' in *Art History, Aesthetics and Visual Studies*, Holly & Moxey (eds.), pp.189–190. Cf. *Visual Culture Reader*, N Mirzoeff (ed.), Routledge, London, 1999.

9. 'Showing Seeing: A Critique of Visual Culture' in *Art History, Aesthetics and Visual Studies*, Holly & Moxey (eds.), p.233. W J T Mitchell, 'Interdisciplinarity and Visual Culture' *The Art Bulletin* 77 (1995) pp.540–4 and 'What is Visual Culture' in *Meaning in the Visual Arts: Views from the Outside*, I Lavin (ed.), Institute for Advanced Study, Princeton N J, 1995.

10. 'Preface' in *Visual Culture*, N Bryson, M A Holly and K Moxey (eds.), Wesleyan University Press, Middletown, Conn., 1994. See also *Visual Theory*, N Bryson, M A Holly and K Moxey (eds.), Polity Press, Cambridge, 1991.

11. *Seen/Unseen*, 'Introduction,' p.1.

12. For one instance of this, see M Kemp, 'Intellectual Ornaments: Style, Interpretation, Function and Society in Some Instruments of Art' in *Intepretation and Cultural History*, J H Pittock and A Wear (eds.), St Martin's Press, 1991.

13. *Seen/Unseen*, p.7.

14. *Visualizations*, p.1.

15. *Visualizations*, p.1. And further: 'I believe [...] that the deep structures of intuition with which we have been endowed by nature and nurture stand in a non-arbitrary relationship to definable elements in the structure and behaviour of the physical world.'

16. See M Podro, *The Critical Historians of Art*, Yale University Press, New Haven and London, 1982, pp.9–11 for a concise account, and for more detail his *The Manifold of Perception: Theories of Art from Kant to Hildebrand*, Clarendon Press, Oxford, 1972, Chapter II.

17. Here I am referring to points made in 'Artists on Science, Scientists on Art' *Nature* 434 (March 2005) pp.308–9.

Matthew Landrus

Leonardo and theories of beauty

Sense is a ratio. Aristotle, *De Anima* 426b

Leonardo's theories about beauty appear in various ways throughout his notebooks and particularly in his *Treatise on Painting*. Even when there is no direct reference to *bellezza*, *symmetria* or *harmonia*, these associations may be assumed in his discussions about better inventions or expressions. Hence the ubiquitous nature of theories of beauty in his work makes any summary assessment difficult. In the *Treatise on Painting's* 'paragone' (comparison of the arts), for example, Leonardo refers to a contemporary story of King Mathias' lecture to the poet that poetry 'does not satisfy the mind of the listener or the viewer in the same way as the proportionality of the very beautiful (*bellissime*) parts composing the divine beauty (*bellezze*) of this face before me' [in a painting].[1] The king offers an opinion as well as an objective judgement regarding specific qualities. Secondly, in a statement nearly eighteen years later, around 1508–10, Leonardo warns against judgements that may not be objective. He proposed instead that, 'when judgement disdains the work this is a perfect sign,' that this objective judge – the painter – 'will produce few works, although these will be of such quality that men will stop in admiration to contemplate their perfection.'[2] Thirdly, he also recommends that one avoid automimesis by making an eclectic composite of numerous studies, 'to collect the good features from many beautiful faces, but let their beauty be confirmed by public renown than by your own judgement.'[3] Finally, in essence, he often tried to specify a theory that was itself part of an objective 'science' of painting, stating: 'O marvellous science, you keep alive the transient beauty of mortals and you have greater permanence than the works of nature.'[4] Yet these four approaches that one may associate with theories of beauty in the *Treatise on Painting* interpret different theories of the proportionality, divinity, objective judgement, eclectic composite, and 'science' of beauty. What, however, may be central to Leonardo's theories of beauty and how did he put into practice what he discussed?   ¶   To begin with, he referred to beauty in much the same way Marsilio Ficino (1433–99) referred to it: that beauty 'pertains rather to the sight than to the hearing.'[5] The primacy of sight, along with its immediate link to the soul and its interpretation of proportional harmony, was fundamental to Leonardo's claim in his *paragone* that painting was a liberal art. Thus his interests in the Neoplatonic approach, in his earliest statements for a *paragone*, around 1492, signify his contact with the Florentine debates on classifications of the arts at that time. Authors of the debates included Ficino, Poliziano, and Savonarola. During 1490–92, Savonarola (1452-98) lectured on and published *De divisione scientium*, which included the science of perspective within the Quadrivium; Angelo Poliziano (1454–94) published his *Panepistemon* (1491), which defined painting, sculpture, and architecture within a category of mechanical arts that was parallel to the poetic arts; and as Claire Farago notes, 'Ficino proposed an unprecedented classification of painting, sculpture, and architecture among the liberal arts' in a letter to the astron-omer, Paul of Middleburg. Hence Florentine Neoplatonism may have encouraged Leonardo to produce written arguments that would eventually form a *paragone*.[6] In Milan he also had direct access to a number of Florentine associates who were aware of the intellectual climate in Florence.   ¶   Still, it is unlikely that he studied these particular debates at length. The fact that such debates might have inspired him is enough to show the shared concern for aesthetic approaches among late fif-teenth century theologians, philosophers, poets, and painters. Also important to the re-evaluation of the arts at this time was the ability to include in one's proofs a broad range of approaches, including associations with the soul and mind, medieval faculty psychology, Greek symmetry, Roman rhetoric, Euclidian geometry, Arabic natural optics, the science of perspective optics, musical harmony, pictorial *belleze*, poetic theology (*theologia poetica*), concentrating on the proportion theories relative to these approaches. To Leonardo and his contemporaries, this broad range of ap-proaches was often considered naturally interconnected and multidisciplinary, governed by proportional laws similar to all of these approaches. Nonetheless, it was Leonardo, along with Francesco Melzi, the editor of his Treatise on Painting, who took the relatively unprecedented step to feature Proportion Theory, and in so doing, a theory of beauty, so prominently in their comparison of the arts. ¶ Even if Leonardo opposed Neoplatonist opinion that the mortal body was the soul's 'abysmal dwelling,' he tried to find solutions to Neoplatonist problems such as automimesis.[7] He apparently had Ficino's 1482 *Theologia platonica sive de immortalitate animarum*, which he seems to have titled *De Immortalità d'anima* in his book list of 1490–3 (of Codex Atlanticus folio 559r/210r-a).[8] Moreover, a friend of his during the 1470s and part of 1480, Bernardo di Simone Canigiani, was a pupil of Ficino.[9] A reference by Ficino to beauty, or *bellezze* (proportional beauties), as more visual than auditory is a sign of changing attitudes toward this judgement. During the fifteenth century, 'beauty' had gradually become more of an issue of what Alberti (1404–72) termed a *concinnitas* (indissoluble harmony) of architecture, rather than an issue of audible harmonic proportion of a Pythagorean kind. As noted by Martin Kemp, quoting Alberti: '*concinnitas*, "the spouse of the soul and of reason," arose when the three visual properties – number, outline (or shape) and position (or location) – manifested an indissoluble harmony or proportional correspondence in the parts and in the whole, 'so that nothing may be added, taken away or altered, but for the worse.'[10] Furthermore, the Italian concept of *bellezza*, in terms of the Greek *symmetria* or *harmonia*, or the Latin *pulchritudo* or *bellus*, had become more narrowly defined, referring to a greater range of more specific characteristics not necessarily limited – as in antiquity – to the body of a person or that of a building.[11] The Latin term, *proportio* (proportion), was also equivalent in the fifteenth century to the Greek term, *analogia* (the arithmetical or geometric comparison of phenomena or ideas.[12] After Cicero (106–43 BCE), concepts of harmonic, arithmetic, and geometric forms of proportion combined in such a way that *proportio* referred generally to the *symmetria*, *harmonia*, and *pulchritudo* of visible or audible forms, whereas *analogia* was increasingly a distinct form of *proportio* in what were considered metaphysical problems of arithmetic and geometry.[13] This is one reason that predominantly visual proportion theories appeared so often in Leonardo's work before 1496, when he had a greater interest in non-mechanical geometry and arithmetic. Before 1496, his work involves visual, philosophical, and mechanical draughting proportion theories, more than the metaphysical *analogia* and the *proportio* of what he termed *quantita continua* (geometry) and *quantita discontinua* (arithmetic).   ¶   A sign of the medieval shift in approach to proportional *pulchritudo* is in the reference of Albertus Magnus (c. 1193/1206–80) to beauty *in spritualibus* and *in essentialibus*, in addition to its previous attribution, *in corporibus*.[14] This makes clear a spiritual component (as associated with the corporeal and how something is itself) that one can also derive from Thomas Aquinas' (c. 1225–74) approach to proportionality in the works of Plato and Aristotle. Aquinas emphasizes the appeal of proportional beauty to the incorporeal intellect and soul as part of the cognitive process:

> *Beauty and goodness in a thing are identical fundamentally, for they are based upon the same thing, namely, the form; and this is why goodness is praised as beauty. But they differ logically, for goodness properly relates to appetite (the appetite being a kind of movement towards a thing). On the other hand, beauty relates to a cognitive power, for those things are said to be beautiful which please when seen. Hence beauty consists in due proportion, for the senses delight in things duly proportioned, as in what is like them, because the sense too is a sort of reason, as is every cognitive power. Now, since knowledge is by assimilation, and likeness relates to form, beauty properly belongs to the nature of a formal cause.[15]*

Relating beauty/proportionality to a cognitive power, Aquinas supported his thesis in the *Summa Theologica* that man's incorporeal (spiritual) intellect, rather than his body, is more analogous to God than the claim in *Genesis* 1:26 of man's corporeal image resembling that of God. By contrast, Vitruvius (c. 80/70 – after 15 BCE) associated proportional beauty clearly with the physical world, stating that 'Architecture depends on order (*taxis*), arrangement (*diathesis*), eurythmy, (*eurythmia* or 'proportion') symmetry, propriety, and economy (*oeconomia*)' (Bk 1, Ch 2), and that 'in the human body there is a kind of symmetrical harmony (*symmetros est eurythmiae qualitas*) between forearm, foot, palm, finger, and the other small parts' (Bk 3, Ch

1).[16] ¶ Toward the end of the fifteenth century there were narrower definitions for beauty, such that symmetry was normally used only to describe visual beauty, and harmony was normally used to describe audible beauty. Ficino stated, for example, that:

We do indeed perceive the reflection of divine beauty with our eyes and mark the resonance of divine harmony with our ears – those bodily senses which Plato considers the most perceptive of all … It is necessary for him who is so moved not only to desire that supernal beauty but also wholly to delight in its appearance which is revealed to his eyes. For Nature has so ordained that he who seeks anything should also delight in its image; but Plato holds it the mark of a dull mind and corrupt state if a man desires no more than the shadows of that beauty nor looks for anything beyond the form his eyes can see … Elsewhere he describes this love as the ardent desire of a soul, which in a way is dead in its own body, while alive in another.[17]

Leonardo was likely aware of this specific kind of interpretation of the soul's reception of the divine beauty of images and the divine harmony of sounds, stating Ficino's basic argument around 1490–2 in his *Treatise on Painting*, chapters 23 and 27:

Your soul would … enjoy the beneficence of its eyes, the windows of its dwelling … and … receive the species of cheerful places. [23]

Our soul is composed of harmony, and that harmony is only generated in those instants when the proportionality of objects is seen and heard. [27, quoting King Mathias][18]

To see how Leonardo put Neoplatonic theory to use one need only look to his *Last Supper*. The pictorial impact of Christ's message, 'woe unto that man by whom he is betrayed!' emanates in the form of a perspective construction from the vanishing point at his right temple, rather than – as had been popular in the fifteenth century – from a location like his mouth or any other significant part of the painting. This vanishing point points to the position of the soul in the *sensus communis* at the centre of the brain, and the soul at this point in space and time effectively informs, receives and governs everything in the painting. In this way Leonardo reveals Christ's role in the unfolding tragedy, the moment when those at the table must confront their own true identities, the complex breakthrough Aristotle referred to as a unity of *perip-*

eteia (reversal of expectations) and *anagnorisis* (recognition of one's own identity).[19] This theatrical expression, or *ut pictura poesis*, is both Eucharist and 'strife' among apostles to identify the traitor in Luke 22:24, connecting the painting specifically with Luke's extended account.[20] Moreover, Leonardo incorporates the usual poetic metaphor, pivoting the painting and its actions on the *tempia* (at the side of the head), as well as on the *tempio* (temple of the body).[21] The Vitruvian symmetrical harmony of the body and temple applies here as well as the association of *tempia* with *tempero* (to develop in due proportion), and *temperi* (at the right time). Thus within the symmetrical harmony of Christ's physical body his incorporeal intellect sets the tempo for a painting arranged according to musical proportions of an octave, a fifth and a fourth (see FIG 1).[22] Centering the composition in this way was an early consideration for the painting, in the form of a geometric diagram in the centre of Windsor folio 12542r (redrawn on FIG 2 and 3). At the base of this circle, the width of an arc and triangles happen to match the width of the *Last Supper* coffers at the position of the architrave, such that a square constructed with this arc width perfectly frames the central space of the painting, and the draughted circle and triangles match the space of the refectory wall as well as its centre point at Christ's right temple. The theory of beauty Leonardo uses here is that the *Last Supper* is symmetry and harmony, and its rhetorical function as a tragedy is expressed in its form. Raphael possibly recognised a Neoplatonic approach in the *Last Supper*, honoring Leonardo by painting him as Plato in the *School of Athens* twelve years later. Possibly considering Leonardo's mural, Raphael centered his fresco in much the same way the *Last Supper* was centered (FIG 4). ¶ By 1508, Leonardo was particularly interested in the 'entirely mental,' relatively Platonic, nature of the visible science of geometry. His discussion in MS. F, folio 59r (c. 1508) of his own diagram of a geometrical proof, responds to what he claims to be a non-geometric/mechanical proof attributed to Plato. He argues that his was not designed in the way that Plato's diagram was designed, that is mechanically (non-geometrically), with 'the use of instruments of the compass and the straight edge ... but [this] ... is all mental, and as a consequence, geometrical.'[23] Kemp notes, with reference to this passage, that 'nowhere was Leonardo more a classicist in the Renaissance sense than in his late geometry.'[24] This interest in intellectual geometry, and thus divine beauty, echoed the sermons of Ficino in the Florence Cathedral after 1473, which also profoundly influenced the Polliauolo brothers, Botticelli, Michelangelo, Raphael, and, it would seem, Leonardo.[25] The painter or sculptor who deserved a status greater than that of a carpenter was one who invented visual resemblances of the divine world and thereby offered visual reminders to the soul of its own divinity.[26] ¶ Perhaps no other source was more influential on Leonardo's Treatise on Painting than Alberti's *De pictura*, though Alberti avoided discussions of the role of the soul in the interpretation of harmony or beauty.[27] In *De pictura*, as Cecil Grayson notes, painting is treated as an entirely physical 'expression of the whole man and of his ethical and spatial relationship with his environment,' and in *De statua*, there is 'no trace ... of any metaphysical meaning ascribed to proportion.'[28] Ficino and Aquinas, as Leonardo might have known, held that the soul received and interpreted divine harmonies. Returning to Leonardo's *paragone*, chapters 23 and 27 noted above, it is apparent that these discussions do not appear in Alberti's text, though they may bear some relationship to the writings of Ficino and Aquinas. ¶ Alberti's words, *anima* and *mente*, according to Grayson, denote the physical 'soul' and 'mind' on earth, the two terms referring to a similar moral and rational function of the mind.[29] Leonardo, though he usually referred to *mente* as the mind, referred to the *anima* both as a physical component of the body in some statements, and as a metaphysical entity in other statements, perhaps as a result of the profound general influence of Neoplatonism in northern Italy at the end of the fifteenth century. Leonardo might have read Alberti's statement that Apelles' visual narrative of *Calumny* 'seizes the imagination when described in words, how much beauty and pleasure do you think it presented in the actual painting of that excellent artist?'[30] Around 1490–92, Leonardo included this concept of painting as mute poetry in his notes for a *paragone*, stating that:

> *Painting is a mute poem and poetry is a blind painting, and both proceed by imitating nature as far as their powers make it possible, and many moral habits can be demon-*

strated through both of them, as did Apelles with his Calumny. Yet a harmonic propor-
tion results from painting because it serves the eye, a sense more noble than the ear,
which is the object of poetry (chapter 21). [31]

In this case, he adds to the traditional interpretation of *Calumny* the importance of harmonic proportion in the ability of a painting to move the viewer in a single moment. Late fifteenth century painters associated this story with the first impulse in the creative process, which was described by Ficino in his *Platonic Theology*: 'The whole field appeared in a single moment to Apelles and aroused in him a desire to paint.'[32] It seems likely that Leonardo considered this statement in his copy of *De Immortalità d'anima*, and it can be safely assumed that he and Ficino shared a common interest in the comment of Aquinas that sight, 'because it does not involve physical change on the part of either object or organ is the most spiritual, the highest of the senses, with the widest range of objects.'[33] In this and *Columny* we have a basic principle among Leonardo's theories of beauty: that the painter has a responsibility to use the liberal art of painting to engage one's appreciation of all liberal arts, to render symmetry and harmony with this 'marvellous science' and mute poetry, to draught divine proportions that resonate in the eye and ear of mind, body and spirit.

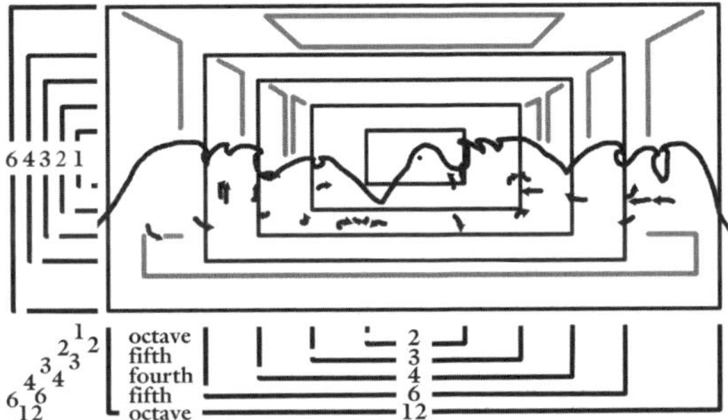

FIGURE 1 Diagram Leonardo's *Last Supper*.

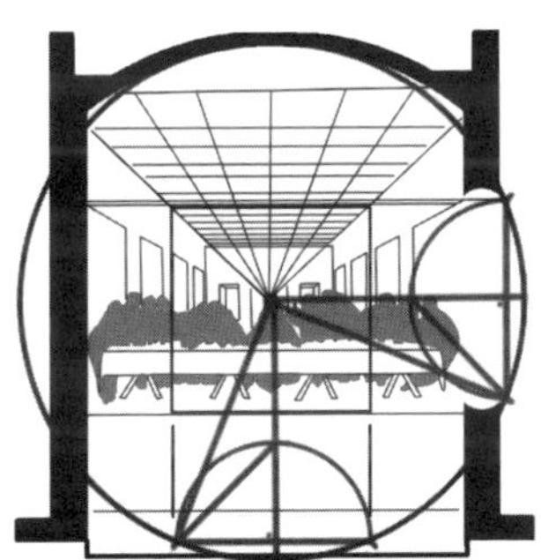

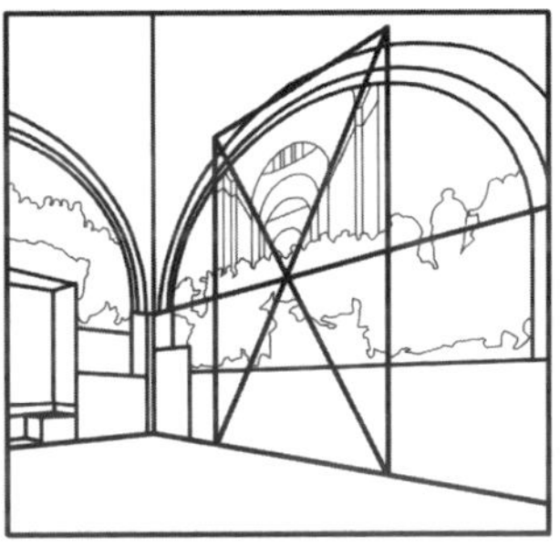

FIGURE 4 Diagram of Raphael's Stanza della Segnatura with the *School of Athens*.

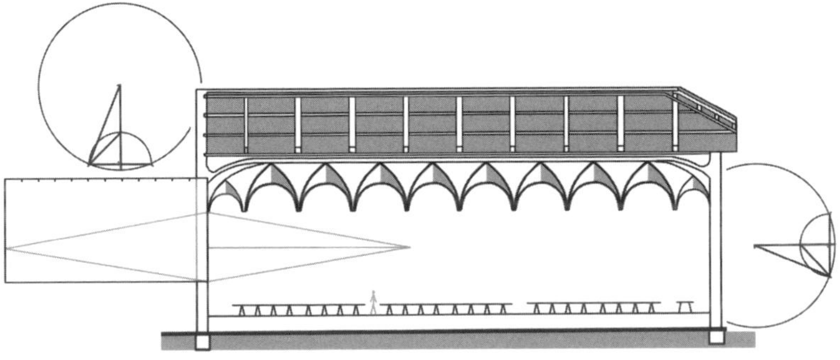

FIGURE 2 (above) & 3 (above left) The geometrical study on Windsor f.12542r superimposed onto diagrams of the refectory of Santa Maria delle Grazie, measuring 60 x 15 *braccia*.

1. Codex Urbinas, 15r, c. 1490–92, in *Leonardo on Painting*, M Kemp and M Walker (eds.), Yale, New Haven CT, 1989, p.26.

2. Codex Urbinas, 131v, c. 1508–10, *Leonardo on Painting*, p.97.

3. Codex Urbinas, 51r, MS A 107r, c.1492, *Leonardo on Painting*, p.204. This issue is also addressed in M Kemp, "'Ogni dipintore dipinge se:" a Neoplatonic echo in Leonardo's art theory,' in *Cultural Aspects of the Italian Renaissance, Essays in honor of Paul Oskar Kristeller*, Manchester University, Manchester, 1976, pp.311–23. F Zöllner, "'Ogni pittore dipinge sé," Leonardo da Vinci and Automimesis,' in *Der Künstler über sich in Seinem Werk*, Internationales Symposium der Bibliotheca Hertziana, Rom, 1989, M Winner (ed.), V C H, Weinheim, 1992, pp.137–160.

4. Codex Urbinas, 16v, c. 1490–92, *Leonardo on Painting*, p.35.

5. M Ficino, in *Plotini Epitome ... operum philosophicorum omnium libri liv.*, cum Lat. M Ficini interpretatione e commentatione, Basil, 1561, p.1576

6. See C Farago, *Leonardo da Vinci's Paragone: A Critical Interpretation*, E J Brill, Leiden, 1992, pp.68–72, 289–302.

7. M Ficino, letter to Giovanni Cavalcanti, 'Serious words to Giovanni. The soul perceives after death, and much more clearly than when in the body,' in *The Letters of Marsilio Ficino*, Shepheard-Walwyn, London, 1978, Vol.I, p.80.

8. See *Leonardo da Vinci, Il Codice Atlantico*, A Marinoni (ed.), Tomo II, Florence, Guinti, 2002, p.1096. E Solmi, *Scritti vinciani*, La nuova Italia, Firenze, 1976 [1908], pp.542–3. *Notebooks of Leonardo da Vinci*, J P Richter (ed.), New York, Dover, 1970 [1883] Vol II., p.444. *The Literary Works of Leonardo da Vinci, Compiled and Edited from the Original Manuscripts by Jean Paul Richter, Commentary by Carlo Pedretti*, C. Pedretti (ed.), University of California, Berkeley, 1977, Vol.II, pp. 353–56.

9. CA 18r/4r-b, c.1480. *Notebooks of Leonardo*, §1553, p.465. Solmi, pp 542–3.

10. *Leon Battista Alberti On Painting*, Cecil Grayson (trans.), M Kemp (intro.), Penguin, London, 1991, p.8.

11. For the change in definitions, see W Tatarkiewicz, *History of Aesthetics*, Vol. 2, Mouton, The Hague, 1962.

12. Varro (116–27 BCE) notes the equivalence of *proportio* and *analogia* in: *De Lingua Latina*. Cicero appears to have been the first to associate the *analogia* with the Latin *proportio*, particularly in his translation of the Timaeus IV:13. See K C Reiley, *Studies in the philosophical Terminology of Lucretius and Cicero*, PhD thesis, New York University, 1909, p.13.

13. See notes on this by Archytas (428–347 BCE) in H Lyttkens, 'The Analogy between God and the World,' *Upsalla Universitets Årsskrift*, 1953, p.16, n.7.

14. Tatarkiewicz, p.166.

15. *Summa Theologica*, London, 1911, I, Q.5, Art.4, ad.1.

16. *The Ten Books of Architecture*, M H Morgan (trans.), Wissenschaftliche Buchgesellschaft, Darmstadt, 1964, p.13.

17. From a letter by Ficino to Peregrino Agli, dated 1st December 1457, in *The Letters of Marsilio Ficino*, Vol.1, pp.44–45.

18. C Farago, pp.224–5, 234–5.

19. Aristotle's *Poetics*, 1452[a]30–32 and 24–29.

20. Compare Luke 22:16–38, Matthew 26:21–29, Mark 14:18–25 and John 13:21–29.

21. He also referred to temples (*tempie*) of the head in MS. A109r, and on Windsor Royal Library folio 19058r.

22. *See* M Landrus, 'The Proportions of Leonardo's *Last Supper*,' *Raccolta Vinciana* 32, Sforza Castle, Milan, 2007.

23. *The Manuscripts of Leonardo da Vinci in the Institute de France, Manuscript F*, J Venerella (trans.), Castello Sfrozesco, Milan, 2002, p.112.

24. M Kemp, *Leonardo da Vinci, The Marvellous Works of Nature and Man*, Harvard, Cambridge MA, 1981, p.298.

25. *See* S Meltzoff, *Botticelli, Signorelli, and Savonarola*, Olschki, Florence, 1987. M Kemp, review of S Melzoff, 'Botticelli ...' in *Times Literary Supplement* 4486 (24 March 1989) p. 312. C Farago, pp.70-72. P O Kristeller, *Eight Philosophers of the Italian Renaissance*, Stanford, Palo Alto CA, 1964, pp.25–53.

26. *See The Letters of Marsilio Ficino*, Vol.1, p.20.

27. *See* C Farago, pp.22, 49, 61–63, 88, 100–101, 121, 294, 314–315, 329–31, 340–46, 368–71, 385–86, 395–402, 412–21. M Kemp in L B Alberti, *On Painting*, C Grayson (trans.), M Kemp (intro.), Penguin, London, 1991, p.23.

28. C Grayson, *Studi su Leon Battista Alberti*, Olschki, Florence, 1998, pp.297 & 307.

29. L B Alberti, *I primi tre libri della Famiglia* [1434], F C Pellegrini (transc.), Sansoni, Florence, 1946, pp.194–8. C Grayson, pp.138–9. M Kemp in: *On Painting*, p.25.

30. Chapter 53, C Grayson (trans.), p.89.

31. C Farago, pp.216–19.

32. Book III: 1 of *Opera Omnia*, Basil, Henricpetri, 1576, Bottega d'Erasmo, Turin, 1983, R Marcel (ed.), Vol.1, pp.118, 135.af.

33. *Summa Theologiae*, 1a.78. art.3 reply, Blackfriars edition, London, Eyre and Spottiswoode, 1964, 11:33. Farago, p.75. D Summers, *The Judgement of Sense*, Cambridge University, Cambridge, 1987, pp.32–42.

Matt Gatton

First light: inside the palaeolithic camera obscura

A few years ago, realist painter Madison Cawein found inexpensive studio space in a long-empty boarded-up factory building. As he wandered through the building one day he poked his head inside a darkened room and saw clouds floating across the floor, cars driving across the ceiling, and workers scurrying around a construction project hovering upside-down on the wall. He had not entered an alternate dimension nor had he inhaled too much mineral spirit vapour; he had, in fact, stumbled upon a camera obscura (literally 'chamber of darkness'). A small hole in a painted-over window allowed in a beam of light, which projected an inverted moving image of the outside world onto the surfaces inside the room. Though Cawein understood the physics at play, the experience was nonetheless magical. Coming across a randomly formed camera obscura, though uncommon, is not as rare an event as one might suppose. There are likely a number of people today happening upon projected images in cargo trucks, boats, houses, and buildings. This is the way it has always been. We have anecdotes throughout written history that describe these camera obscuras, from holes in the curtains of contemporary homes to tenth-century Arabian tents to 5th century BC Chinese pagodas. Camera obscuras happen because of the manner in which people enclose themselves from the outside world. We are not anatomically adapted to many of the climates we inhabit, so we have made do by building living spaces to protect us from the elements. Our dwellings are naturally dimmer than the sunlit world outside and before the invention of the glass window-pane our interior spaces were dimmer still. The contrast between a bright outside and a dim inside is the foundation of camera obscura formation. All that is left is for the agents of material deterioration – weather, storms, rot, heat, cold, birds, termites, ants, bees, mice, pets, children, and teenagers – to make a small opening. Holes happen, camera obscuras happen.   ¶   This simple camera obscura principle would evolve into a manufactured object fashioned of wood and metal with a fine lens, mirror, and ground glass, which would, in time, launch the medium of photography in AD 1839. Many people think of a camera obscura as this precise device of human engineering, unaware of the ancient and accidental nature of the hole-in-a-tent-wall-type camera obscura. The term camera obscura unfortunately applies to both, fuelling misunderstanding. The concept of a camera obscura as a fabricated tool and our penchant for heroification have led to the ascribing of the invention of the camera obscura to various scholarly inventors. The truth is that humans can no more invent a camera obscura than we can invent sunlight. A camera obscura, in the simplest sense of the term, is not a human creation but rather a by-product, the forces of optical physics acting in a predictable manner. For as long as we have made shelter, camera obscuras have occurred coincidentally.　¶　In the western tradition, the Renaissance saw remarkable advances in lens and mirror quality and clarity, spawning a variety of optical aids for artists, as chronicled by Martin Kemp, the leading authority on the science of art. Based on textual evidence, Kemp put the date at AD 1550 for the earliest mention of the use of a lens as the aperture of a camera obscura. Tapping into Kemp's expertise, artist David Hockney experimented with lenses and mirrors and put forth the idea that artists began using optical aids at an earlier date, c. 1420–30 AD at the time of a relatively rapid artistic transition from rudimentary flatness to full accurate proportion, perspective, and foreshortening. Hockney's hypothesis spawned a controversy in the art historical community and he was assailed from many quarters, not only from those who felt he was inferring that great Renaissance masters were cheaters, but also from historians and scientists who were certain that the focal lengths and optical clarity of the lenses and mirrors that Hockney suggested were not available at such an early a date. Salvos of accusations and recriminations flew back and forth. And some may have come away from the controversy with the idea that no lenses means no images. Though lenses and mirrors are advantageous, making the image brighter, they are not necessary. A small hole will do. Hockney's mirror-lens based move, 120 year backward in time, is but the blink of an eye when compared to the prehistoric depth of the hole-in-the-wall sort of camera obscura. Tracing projected images inside dark spaces is so very simple that it goes much, much deeper into human history.

Palaeolithic tents as camera obscuras

Though the peoples of the Palaeolithic are commonly referred to as cavemen, they actually did not live deep inside caves, but survived harsh climates in simple animal hide tents, which were invariably situated in daylight settings – just inside a cave mouth or tucked under a rock overhang or in the open air. We are not bats and cannot live where we cannot see. The archaeological record is replete with carefully excavated Palaeolithic habitation sites. The actual physical evidence of these simple shelters is limited to permanent materials like stone and bone. No wooden post or animal hide has been found, because these materials rot over the course of time. But the existence of these perishable elements can easily be established. Postholes prove the existence of wooden poles even in their physical absence. The alignment of the holes and/or anchor stones describes the footprint of the framework, which is understood to have supported animal hides via a plethora of ethnographic parallels. Modern day reconstructions of Palaeolithic tents (made with hides, sinews, stones, and wooden poles) also act as coincidental camera obscuras. Occasional small holes in the opaque but weathered hides allow daylight to stream in and project an image of the outside world. But recognizable images cannot be projected from just any hole, some are too small and others too large, and even an optimum sized hole will only project an image when the sun is at a proper angle, which varies by the time of day and season. Such factors would make projected images seem an almost random occurrence, until someone figured out how to make them.

Portable Palaeolithic engravings as tracings of projected images

The most well known Palaeolithic artworks are deep cave paintings, which have survived because of the environmental stability of the cave – a steady temperature, a complete lack of destructive ultraviolet light, and a near constant air moisture level. But cave painting is only part of the story of Palaeolithic art. Thousands of very odd engravings on small stones and bones have been recovered from hundreds of day-light Palaeolithic habitation sites, the day-to-day living areas where people made their dwellings. This is the great-untold story of Palaeolithic art. These engravings often exhibit jumbles of lines, that when teased apart reveal randomly sized, variably oriented figures, with peculiar repeated and incomplete features, superimpositions, and distortions. And yet for their strangeness, there is a momentary aspect to many of the figures, an unparalleled immediacy like glances in time. Our studio drawing experiments show the distinct line quality of these Palaeolithic engravings is consistent with tracing a moving light image inside a camera obscura.   ¶   The look of any artwork is determined by the artist's choices. The artist decides what to draw and how to draw it; determines which available supplies and tools to use; and opts for techniques that are appropriate to the materials and subject matter – all within a cultural context. There is a circular and limiting factor in these choices: certain tools require specific techniques, and specific techniques require certain tools. Any given artwork is a document of aesthetic decision-making, a map of the artist's path. A visual artist's choice of tools and techniques affects the look of an artwork in the same way a musician's choice of instrument affects the sound of the music.   ¶   Since different artistic methods produce different characteristics, we devised a set of drawing experiments with a group of students to compare the look of three different drawing methods: observation, memory, and the very obscure, almost unheard of, tracing of a moving projected image. In the art studio, the experiments began with students being instructed to draw a bison. No pictures of or visual references to bison were on display in the room and students were given no instruction on how to draw the bison. The next class session, video footage of bison slowly grazing and meandering about a field was projected onto the far wall of the room and students were again instructed to draw bison. Students naturally alternated their gaze between the bison and the drawing paper. While the student's were on break, the projector was flipped over, casting an upside-down image (mimicking the projection inside a camera obscura) on to the wall. When students returned they were instructed to trace the bison. One-by-one, students put their drawing sheets on the wall and attempted to trace the bison as they moved about. ¶ As one might expect, the memory drawings were generally rudimentary, while the observation drawings where more proportional. The tracings, however, took on a completely different look with individual animals depicted with multiple heads, legs, and tails. The light that formed the image overpowered any information on the drawing surface making it nearly impossible for the students to see their lines as they traced. Working with lines that cannot be seen caused strange things happen. The first line was drawn then the head turned, the tail swished, a leg shifted; and the next line was laid over in a new place, accurately documenting the animal's movement. It is also important to note that in our experiments no student drew a nine legged bison from memory or observation; however, repeated features became routine in the moving image tracings. Figures with multiple features that eloquently describe motion have been a characteristic of Palaeolithic art that has long perplexed researchers. ¶ In the memory and observation drawings sessions, no student failed to connect body parts. When drawing an animal on a visible drawing surface, the artist can easily see which sections have been completed and which are left to do. But in the tracing sessions, incomplete outlines and unattached body sections became commonplace. Not being able to see the lines not only made for repeated areas, but also disconnected areas. The projected image tracing method used in the experiments had a definitive impact on the look of the drawings and a resonance with Palaeolithic habitation site engravings. ¶ To illustrate the point, let us look at a demonstration with a small horse as it naturally stands around fending off flies, mosquitoes, and other pests. When we trace the horse's image the lines pile up on different parts of the animal at different times, which yields a multi-legged and multi-headed beast that could be interpreted as a small group of horses (FIG 1). Comparing our illustration with a Palaeolithic engraving from the habitation site of La Marche, which has similar characteristics, it is clear that it could also be one animal at several moments in time (FIG 2). The moving image tracing factors are evident on many other Palaeolithic engravings, including this horse on bone from Laugerie Basse (FIG 3). The odd repetitions, superimposed and disconnected lines, and the element of time give an indication that Palaeolithic people sometimes traced projected images inside their tents.   ¶   In a second round of experiments, students were given small oddly shaped pieces of stiff grey mat board, which mimicked the shape and value of stone, the preferred surface of Palaeolithic engravings. Once each student had made a tracing of the projected image they were instructed to do a second tracing. Most used the other side of the board to do the second tracing, but some drew the second tracing right on top of the first at random angles, because they could not see where the first drawing was against the overpowering projected image.   ¶   Experimenting still further, we set up a room-sized lensless camera obscura on a farm and engraved the cast images of animals on to small stones. The image was quickly outlined before the animal wandered off. The little lines of our engravings were extremely difficult to discern because of the dimness of the space and the overwhelming information in the light of the image, so it did not matter if there was one engraving or one hundred already on the rock. Randomly oriented superimpositions are a product of this method.   ¶   Interestingly, the students sometimes tilted their faux stones out of parallel with the image source, which caused a keystoning distortion in the tracing. We investigated the effect further on the farm. It was most natural for the artist to catch the image with his torso, the engraving stone secured against the body, and the eyes looking down on the inverted image. In this scenario it was advantageous to tilt the stone slightly. The more the stone was tilted the more the image of the animal distorted, the animal's head reducing in size and the stomach bowing downward. It is a distinctly odd distortion that appears in the figures of some portable Palaeolithic engravings and in a more conventionalized form in some deep cave artworks. But let's be clear, there was no camera obscura down in the cave. There is no daylight and no evidence of dwellings in the cave. These deep cave stylized distortions may have a source outside in the day-to-day living areas, the tents, which sometimes acted as camera obscuras.   ¶   The core elements of some Palaeolithic cultures' visual lexicon (repetition, disconnection, movement, superimposition, and distortion) were established in the living spaces where people spent the majority of their time, then occasionally carried into the cave as a longstanding feature of the visual tradition. The characteristics of the engravings in the habitations sites are reiterated in the caves throughout the Upper Palaeolithic. We have unfortunately been under a cavecentric spell, thinking of Palaeolithic art as moving from inside the cave to the outside world, but the archaeological record details the converse process, art holding forth in the outside camps and occasionally moving into the cavern. So when we see the glorious well-preserved art of the deep cave we are catching a glimpse of life on the outside, which should be obvious because there weren't any real living breathing horses or mammoths down in the deep cave, just paintings and engravings of them. The cave artworks are indicators, emblems of a vibrant campsite based visual culture, which from the look of the artworks appears to have included projected images inside the tents. It is our good fortune that caves are natural preservers of ancient art, but we should not be seduced into thinking that they represent the sum total of the Palaeolithic artistic tradition.   ¶   The camera and the cave have striking similarities, they are both dark spaces pierced by light, the tent camera by sunlight from without and the cave by torches and fat burning lamps from within. These points of light cut through the darkness to reveal representations. There is something tantalizing about art production processes that require darkness, because light is so obviously needed to make and see visual art. The use of darkness seems on the surface antithetical, unless the artist has been initiated to the wondrous and subtle conversation between dark and light. Producing art in the dark speaks to the peculiar concept of correlating darkness with visual representation, that the thought process, the logic of Palaeolithic art, had already embraced the visuality of darkness before it entered the cave.

Implications

The availability of moving two-dimensional images inside a tent camera obscura has implications towards the origin of art. We, as a species, appear to have existed for over 150,000 years before making recognizable figurative art, implying that visual communication is more in our nurture than our nature. Our creativity is hard-wired but the form it takes is culturally determined. The trouble for theorists has been finding a way for Palaeolithic people to stumble upon the idea of representation. Though the origins of art are consigned to the realm of complete conjecture, a Palaeolithic tent incidentally acting as a camera obscura offers just such a trigger in an anthropologically, psychologically, and archaeologically feasible way: a physics-based explanation for the idea of depiction. A randomly projected image stands for a real object; it says bison without being a flesh and blood bison, planting the idea of a referent, the true beginning of art. ¶ If these projected images occur randomly across time, why do we not see their tell-tale artistic indicators across more cultures? Because the import of projected light images is far more spiritual and philosophical than aesthetic. Projected images are most often interpreted as spirits, unleashing a cascade of thoughts: 'What is that? It looks so real and yet unreal?' And reflexively: 'What is this? What is existence? What is reality?' The primary function of projected images is to authorise belief in otherworldly realms by offering a glimpse of an alternative plane, by visualizing the invisible. Projected images become a mainstay in early religious practice, the light of ritualized spiritual revelation a near constant. At only a few junctures in time do peoples see aesthetic opportunity in the image, daring to break a strongly-held religious taboo and make the sacred profane. The impact of images on the development of human culture is described in my book, *The (w)hole story: The hidden influence of projected light images,* which covers artistic and religious applications from Palaeolithic to Neolithic to the height of classical antiquity and into the formation of modern religions. Projected images, ephemeral in nature and mesmerizingly haunting, are the key to fully understanding our oldest mythologies, rituals, beliefs, behaviors, artworks, and artifacts. The ancients went into the dark to see the light.

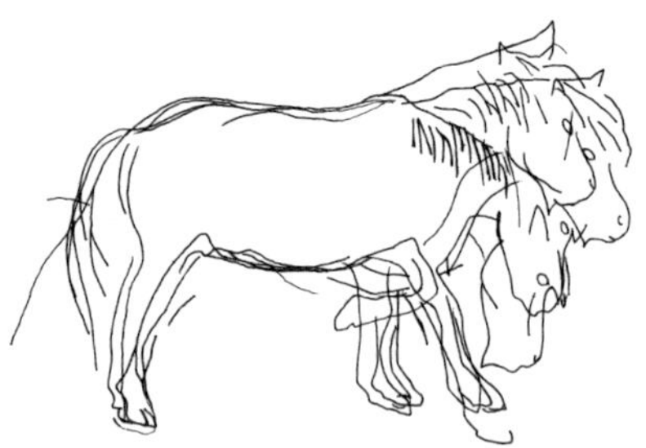

FIGURE 1 Horse, image tracing demonstration, M Gatton, *The overpowering light of the projected image makes the traced lines imperceptible, leading the artist to place lines in different places as the animal moves, thus imparting a time-lapse element to the rendering.*

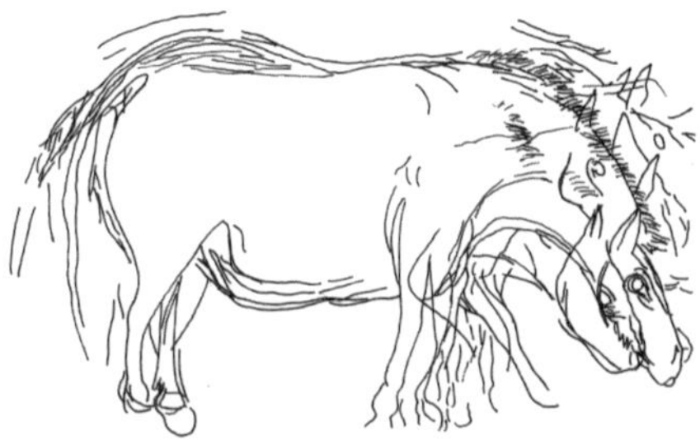

FIGURE 2 Horse, palaeolithic engraving on stone from La Marche, M Gatton after L Pales, *Though often interpreted as a group of horses, the see-through heads, necks, manes, and legs indicate that this may be one horse at several moments in time.*

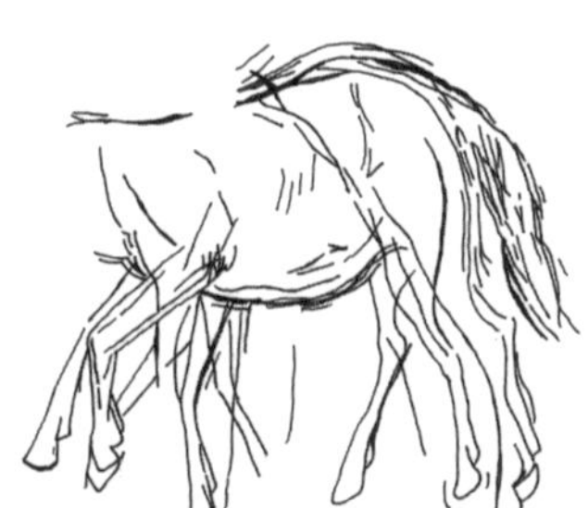

FIGURE 3 Horse, palaeolithic engraving on bone from Laugerie Basse, M Gatton after E Cartailhac, *The ten overlapping legs vividly animate a short period of time and are consistent with the moving image tracing technique.*

Marta de Menezes

The art of being alive

My artwork named *Nature* was made in collaboration with scientists from the laboratory of Professor Paul Brakefield, at the University of Leiden. The work is made up of live butterflies with variations in their wing patterns.[1] The resulting wing patterns had never seen before in nature and were achieved by interfering with the normal developmental mechanisms of the butterflies. The wings are made of normal live cells, without artificial pigments or scars, but designed by an artist. This is an example of something entirely natural, and, at the same time, the outcome of human intervention.[2] As the germline is not affected by any changes, the induced patterns are not transmitted to the offspring. Each modified butterfly is different from any other. The new patterns are due to disappear from nature not to be seen again. This form of art has a finite life span – the life span of a butterfly. It is a form of art that literally lives and dies. ¶ *Functional Portraits* is a project I developed in collaboration with Dr Patricia Figueiredo and scientists at the University of Oxford fMRI Centre. These are portraits representing both the physiognomy of the subject, and the data of the subject's brain function during the performance of an appropriate task. Dr Figueiredo was portrayed while playing a piano piece on a keyboard inside the scanner; Martin Kemp was represented while observing a projection of *The Ambassadors*, by Holbein (FIG 1). ¶ Recently, in my own work I have been interested in a major characteristic of biological systems and their inherent unpredictability. *Proteic Portrait* (2002–2008) (FIG 2) consists of a self portrait made up of the structure of a protein, its three-dimensional shape, combined with an amino-acid sequencing spelling my full name (using the conventional one letter code to represent the amino-acid sequence), the mArta protein:

MARTAISAVELSWVRALRIVEIRWDEMENESESDASILVAGRACA

In Portuguese culture one's name represents a biography in itself: it incorporates the given name, but also the family names of both parents, as well as the husband's name. A computer databases confirmed that there is no known protein with such amino-acid sequence. In order to identify its structure, it was necessary to produce the protein so as to obtain crystals for x-ray diffraction studies. I did this in collaboration with scientists at the Structural Biology Department of Oxford University (Dr Radu Aricescu and Professor Ivonne Jones). Although proteins are not living structures, this project required the use of live organisms. In order to solve the structure of mArta using crystallography it was necessary to produce a large number of copies of mArta. Such production was achieved by designing the gene encoding the information of mArta's sequence, and introducing this gene inside bacteria. The bacteria produced trillions of copies of the protein, subsequently purified from the other bacterial proteins. This is a standard method for the production of synthetic proteins. In this work the artist cannot predict the end result that is exclusively dependent on the molecular interactions established within the mArta protein.[3] ¶ In *DECON: deconstruction, decontamination, decomposition* (2007) (FIG 3), replicas of Piet Mondrian's geometric paintings were made using bacterial support medium. The colours in these paintings are progressively degraded by Pseudomonas putida bacteria. This technology is based on the work by Dr Lígia Martins, at the Instituto de Biologia Química e Biológica in Lisbon, where the project was developed. In her laboratory scientists research biological strategies to degrade highly pollutant textile dyes using bacteria harmless to human beings and to the environment. During the development of *Decon* the optimal conditions that influence bacterial activity were researched in order to adapt the colour degradation rate to the environmental conditions of a museum. The objective was to achieve a slow decomposition of the images during the entire duration of their public exhibition. Thus, the artwork is something literally alive, and as such destined to die and decompose like the rest of us.[4]

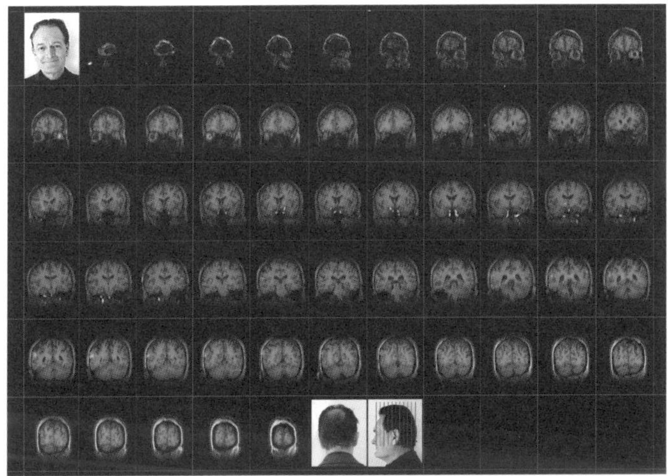

FIGURE 1 *Functional Portraits*, in collaboration with Dr Patricia Figueiredo and scientists at the University of Oxford fMRI Centre. Martin Kemp was represented while observing a projection of *The Ambassadors*, by Holbein.

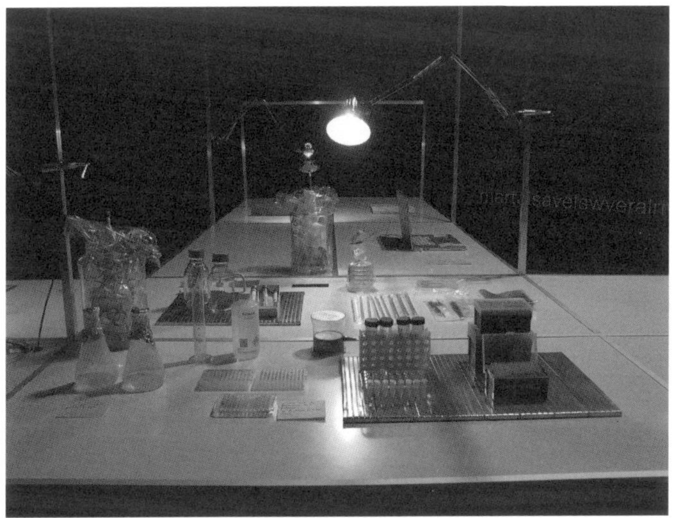

FIGURE 2 *Proteic Portrait* 2002–2008.

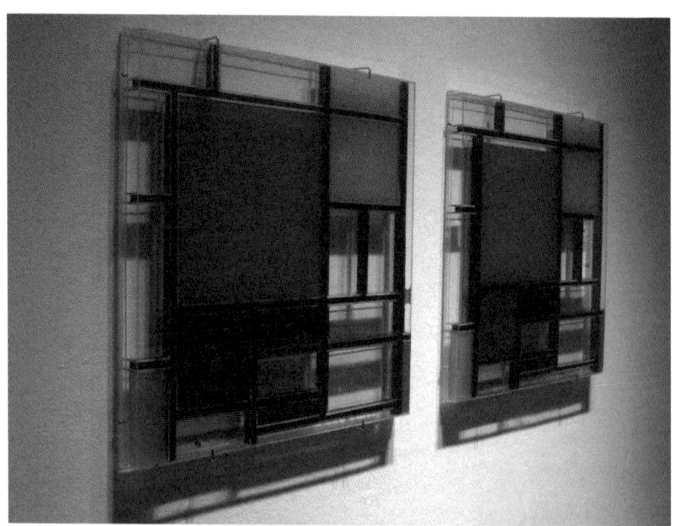

FIGURE 3 *DECON: deconstruction, decontamination, decomposition*, 2007.

1. More information at www.martademenezes.com.

2. M de Menezes, 'The Artificial Natural: Modifying Butterfly Wing Patterns for Artistic Purposes,' *Leonardo 36, no.1*, (2003), pp.29–32.

3. Edited by I Moreira, Proteic Portrait/Retrato Proteico PLP09, 2009, Meiac-Museu Extremeno e Iberoamericano de Arte Contemporaneo.

4. Edited by M de Menezes and J Urbano, Decon:Decontamination, Deconstruction, Decomposition 2009, Private Publication.

Postscript

Martin Kemp

Recent shards of a personal archeology

I have read the draft of this book with a smile on my face. Not just because I am meeting old friends, but because it is full of varied surprises. It seems like fun, for me at least, and I hope for other readers and lookers. Marina Wallace and Assimina Kaniari, as generous and imaginative editors, have gathered together a cast of characters and organised a parade of topics that generate rich series of resonances for readers of different casts of mind. When I was asked about the possibility of assembling such a volume (having expressed doubts about whether it was warranted), I indicated that I would greatly prefer something that was not a standard festschrift – a volume of academic essays 'In Honour of ….' I suggested a collection that reflected the kinds of engagements I have been privileged to enjoy with remarkable people in varied fields of activity. I was hoping to stimulate a creative response from those kind enough to participate. This wish has been delightfully realised. ¶ It is a huge pleasure that historians working in cognate areas, and in some that I had not expected to be associated with, have been joined by practising artists and scientists. My involvement with artists at the cutting edge – artists who really think, who make 'slow art' that repays prolonged contemplation – has been of particular importance to me. It is my conviction that art historians impoverish their range of perception if they do not engage with contemporary art and its practitioners. Artists do not tell us how to look at art from the past – they above all are selective and sometimes contrary witnesses – but they continually open possibilities for fresh acts of seeing that the historian can exercise with critical judgement in the arenas of the past. Not least, I greatly enjoy the company of artists. ¶ There is no obvious thematic unity here in the conventional sense – no set topic to which contributors were forced to make even a passing nod, other than the broad remit of 'acts of seeing.' But I think there is a shared spirit of adventure, and an unwillingness to be constrained by boundaries set by what we think something 'belongs' to. I have always hated the demand for 'relevance.' In the organising of seminars for post-graduate students, I never accepted that a student would not attend one of the papers because 'it is out of my area.' You can never predetermine what insights you will unexpectedly find, or what perspective you might bring to a topic about which you are not well informed. Every discovery begins with the acknowledgement of ignorance. I once said to A S Byatt before a panel on art and science at the Institute for Contemporary Art in London that 'art and science both begin where knowledge ends.' She seemed to like that, and if it is worth her interest, I am happy to repeat it here. ¶ What follows, as an open-ended tailpiece for the volume, are some personal shards, picked up opportunistically from some relatively recent writings. These illustrate two of my enduring concerns. ¶ The first, unsurprisingly, is with the dialogue between what we all too crudely call 'the arts' and 'the sciences.' One essay comes from my very latest column in *Nature*, commissioned in this case as an 'Opinion' to mark 50 years of C P Snow's *Two Cultures*. In its final form it is the result of an expansion from 900 to 1400 words and a good deal of coming and going with my two current editors, Joanne Baker and Anne Blewett. The essentially collaborative nature of the enterprise benefits what eventually appears on the printed page. The other piece presents the opening section of an essay I have produced for a website and book commissioned by the Côa Museum in Portugal. The Museum specialises in Portuguese prehistoric art, but they seem happy to expand their remit into the broadest of visual territories. Their request was to write on 'visual culture.' Dealing with 'visual culture' rather than more narrowly defined aspects of visual history is at once absurdly expansive and specifically demanding on how we approach historical and contemporary artefacts. ¶ The second concern is words. I find foreign languages very difficult, and am still striving to get some measure of control over English. I love the word play of precision against suggestive openness. Both have their vital roles to play if we are to gain access to the past and the present. But they have to be used with due propriety to perform their specific roles in pieces of writing. It has been said in a review of one of my books that I am not interested in 'theory.' What was meant, I think, is that I have not chosen to work specifically with the literary, relativistic, semiotic and deconstructive techniques that have become widespread in art history. My 'theory' resides in questions of perception and cognition with respect to conjoined style and content. I have been consistently involved in modes of visualization and cultural communication. Underlying this 'theory' is a conviction about the interaction between patterns of order and disorder in the visible world with the structuring propensities of our mind. I also have a strong sense of the age-old continuities of human minds. My historical method depends on modes of hypothesis formulation, the taking of evidence, and the offering of conclusions with due respect to limits of what can be said with any measure of confidence. It also rests less systematically with finding verbal ways of evoking the manner in which good art offers a generously ample but non-arbitrary field for interpretation within which each spectator 'can wander at will' (to quote Giovanni Bellini when writing to Isabella d'Este).   ¶   The first piece I offer on this theme of words is the script of a Radio 3 essay on who influenced me as a writer. This choice also acknowledges that I am a 'sports nut.' The others are segments of what I call formatted prose. I dare not call them poetry, because I know nothing of the poet's demanding craft. They were never intended for publication, but Marina extracted one for her section, which has encouraged me to include three others. They are my homage to words, and how difficult they are to use well. Two have also been chosen since they embed some reference to science (perhaps in a rather clumsy manner). They centre on Blenheim Park in Oxfordshire, which, as friends know, has provided me with a vital visual lung after the mental and physical contractions of daily tasks.   ¶   Ultimately, the only words that really matter here, are 'thank you,' offered to all involved in things I treasure greatly.

BOOKS & ARTS

Dissecting The Two Cultures

Fifty years ago today, Charles Percy Snow argued in an influential lecture that the failure of science and the humanities to converse, and the lack of scientists in positions of power, was disastrous for society. In the first of three essays marking this anniversary, **Martin Kemp** contends that the real enemy of understanding is not these 'Two Cultures' but specialization in all disciplines.

"The Two Cultures" is a phrase — like "the corridors of power" — that has seeped into common usage. Divorced from their original context, such phrases tend to become a form of negligent shorthand that allows us to avoid precise thinking. Both were coined by the same author, Charles Percy Snow — one-time physicist, prolific novelist and political climber.

'The Two Cultures' was the title of Snow's hugely influential Rede Lecture at the University of Cambridge, UK, on 7 May 1959. One culture was science; the other was the humanities, as represented by "literary intellectuals". Snow decried what he saw as the total inability of highly educated people to cross a deep rift of mutual incomprehension.

Snow's cultural diagnosis is encapsulated in his famous challenge: "Once or twice I have been provoked and have asked the company [of 'intellectuals'] how many of them could describe the Second Law of Thermodynamics. The response was cold: it was also negative. Yet I was asking something which is about the scientific equivalent of: 'Have you read a work of Shakespeare's?'"

Snow's early career as a research scientist had been aborted in the mid-1930s, when he became disillusioned by having to acknowledge that some of his experimental work on vitamin A — published in *Nature* with Philip Bowden — did not stand up to scientific scrutiny. He subsequently flourished as a novelist, most notably with his 'Strangers and Brothers' series, centered incestuously in the hermetic hothouse of Cambridge academic politics.

He also climbed the ladder of official posts, rising to become parliamentary secretary to the Minister of Technology (1964–1966) in the House of Lords as Baron Snow. He was a major shaper of Prime Minister Harold Wilson's 1963 vision of the "white heat of the technological revolution", and commanded a wide audience both nationally and internationally.

Snow saw applied science as holding the key to a humane future, in terms of a rational understanding of nature but also as the only force that could tackle the problems of well-being in developed and developing countries. Yet 'Luddites' from the humanities still prevailed in the 'corridors of power' — as Snow titled his 1964 novel.

Fuelling the fire

In 1960, as a student newly arrived at the University of Cambridge, I inadvertently encountered the person who was to reignite the controversy sparked by Snow. I saw a haggard figure, shambling across the lawns at Downing College. He was draped in an elderly coat intended for a more ample frame. His leathery neck emerged from a shirt with no tie. Not knowing who he was, I gave him a wide berth, wary of being asked for money.

It transpired that this was the legendary don of English literature and fiery literary critic, Frank R. Leavis. In 1962 Leavis subjected Snow and 'The Two Cultures' to a stinging assault, described not unfairly by philosopher Simon Critchley as "a vicious *ad hominem* attack". Leavis delivered his criticism in the Richmond Lecture that commemorated the last of his 30 years of teaching at Downing College.

Despite his international reputation, Leavis remained, and relished remaining, an outsider in official university circles. Snow, by contrast, had become a heavyweight of the establishment. The cover of the slim volume of Snow's lecture in the university book shop portrayed a well-nourished bulldog of a man in contemplative mode, with dark jacket and neat tie. An obvious insider, in contrast to Leavis the outsider.

Leavis despised Snow's literary works: "as a novelist he doesn't exist; he doesn't begin to exist. He can't be said to know what a novel is." Leavis also dismissed Snow's authority as a cultural guru, regarding him as a mindless sign of the times: "he is a portent in that, being in himself negligible, he has become for a vast public on both sides of the Atlantic a master-mind and a sage … It is ridiculous to credit him with any capacity for serious thinking about the problems on which he offers to advise the world."

Leavis acclaimed great literature as the true guardian of human values: "the judgments the literary critic is concerned with are judgments about life. What the critical discipline is concerned with is relevance and precision in making and developing them." He sided with Blaise Pascal, the French seventeenth-century mathematician and theologian, who declared in his *Pensées* that "physical science will not console me for the ignorance of morality in the time of affliction. But the science of ethics will always console me for the ignorance of the physical sciences."

For Leavis, science — and the technological society it was spawning — was devoid of humane values. He insisted on the need for other kinds of concern, "entailing forethought, action and provision about the human future". To speak of human well-being only "in terms of productivity, material standards of living, hygienic and technological progress" was morally bankrupt. Leavis was witnessing with horror what he saw as the beginning of a takeover by dreaded technocrats, the apocalyptic results of which had been portrayed by George Orwell in his 1949 novel *Nineteen Eighty-Four*.

False divide

Viewed historically, Snow's way of setting up the debate about the two cultures was founded on a false comparison between knowledge of Shakespeare and thermodynamics. The roots

> "In almost all countries, a gulf of understanding has opened up by the time students enter university."

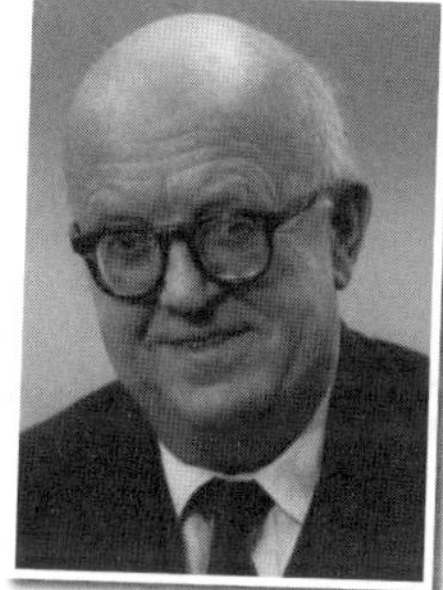

Science stalwart: Charles Percy Snow.

R. COLEMAN, BARON STUDIOS/NATIONAL PORTRAIT GALLERY, LONDON

of this mistaken comparison were laid when knowledge in all forms of learning started to become specialized and professionalized, reaching an apogee when disciplines were institutionalized in the nineteenth century. The establishment of societies was not limited to the sciences and technologies. We can set, for instance, the founding of the Royal College of Veterinary Surgeons in 1844 beside that of the Government School of Design (later to become the Royal College of Art) in 1837.

Since then, the general aspects of high culture have continued to engage professionals in the sciences and humanities to similar degrees. A 2006 study from University College London showed that scientists are only a little less likely to watch a Shakespeare play than their counterparts in the humanities. Specialized research in the humanities is another matter. All academic subjects have become 'laboratory' pursuits with respect to their specialized techniques and vocabularies. Snow's poser about the second law of thermodynamics would be better matched against a narrower question in literary studies, such as asking what is meant by deconstruction as practised by the philosopher Jacques Derrida.

On re-reading the Rede and Richmond lectures today, I am struck by how they are very much of their time. It is difficult to disentangle the personal animosity, the citing of anecdotal experiences and the academic politics from the real issues.

Perhaps the best statement of what was and remains at stake came in Snow's later essay 'The Two Cultures: A Second Look', first published in *The Times Literary Supplement* in 1963: "Persons educated with the greatest intensity we know can no longer communicate with each other on the plane of their major intellectual concern. This is serious for our creative, intellectual and, above all, our normal life. It is leading us to interpret the past wrongly, to misjudge the present, and to deny our hopes of the future. It is making it difficult or impossible for us to take good action."

But we should also recall, above all in the light of current financial and ecological crises, Leavis's insistence on the inadequacy of defining human 'progress' in terms of the implementation of technologies that have been seen as delivering endless economic growth.

The issue does not involve two monolithic 'cultures' of science and humanities. It is about the narrow specialization of all disciplines and wider understanding. I wonder how many biologists could answer Snow's test question, especially in the light of modern physics.

Literary legend: Frank R. Leavis.

I suspect that most scholars in the humanities would fare little better with the Derrida test.

The problem is educational. There is certainly a division between 'sciences' and 'humanities', but the categories are too general to be useful in formulating any plan of action. It is the perceived need for intense specialization of any kind — in history or physics, in languages or biology — that needs to be tackled. Levels of early specialization vary across the world, but in almost all countries, a gulf of understanding has opened up by the time students enter university.

What is needed is an education that inculcates a broad mutual understanding of the nature of the various fields of research, so that we might recognize where their special competence and limitations lie. To paraphrase Christ from the Bible, it is a case of 'render unto science the things that are the sciences' and 'render unto humanities the things that are the humanities'. It is equally important not to render more to each than is warranted. The trick is to do this in the public arena, using well-informed judgement over what belongs and does not belong to each.

Snow's concern about the rift between science and the humanities is real and urgent. But so are Leavis's questions about the terms on which we can arrive at a humane definition of progress. ∎

Martin Kemp is emeritus professor in history of art at the University of Oxford, Oxford, UK.

See Editorial, page 10.

33

This article was first published in Nature on 7th May 2009

Introductory sections from 'Visual Culture – a personal interpretation and a case study,' for the website of the Côa Museum in Portugal, May 2009

Any item produced by human beings involves some element of choice in how that thing should look; that is to say its making involves conscious or unconscious choices about its 'design.' Accordingly the range of objects that could potentially fall under the embrace of 'visual culture' is vast. Indeed, there is hardly anything that we make which does not involve some conscious or unconscious element of visual choice. In practice, the historian is almost bound to select objects for study that speak of elaborate and non-routine intentions (implicit or explicit) on behalf of the makers. Those things that are most directly engaging me at this moment as I write this in my study – my Macintosh computer, my mobile phone, the desk, the Aeron chair on which I sit – are all obviously 'designed' in the conventional sense. I am surrounded by framed photographs, positioned so that they look 'right.'   ¶   Looking at the screen of my computer, I can tell that interface with the Microsoft Word software also has been designed to convey a suitably high-tech look. We would be surprised to find that the toolbars have a hand-made appearance. I choose to type in a traditional Times font, which has a certain 'literary' feel to it. Scientists and 'techies' generally tend to like sans serif fonts, with their blunter functional appearance. I wonder what font this essay will be given on the web. If it is not my original font, the message will feel just that bit different.   ¶   Moving out from our personal ambience of visual culture at a particular moment, we can extend our interest into a wider range of different collectives – by place, time, social group or whatever – to discern the characteristic elements in that collective's visual culture, looking especially at those elements or combinations that seem to separate that culture from others. During the 20th century we increasingly corralled our attention to a society's visual culture into a series of more or less separate enclosures. ('Corralled' is here used with reference to the 'corrals' or pens into which animals are herded). Faced with this narrow corralling, I feel tempted to quote one of my mentors, Sir Ernst Gombrich, whose range of intellectual engagements was enormously wide. When asked to define his 'field,' he responded that 'donkeys have fields.' ¶ The history of art conventionally came to deal with things recognisable as 'Fine Art,' in which the high aim of 'aesthetic excellence' was a prime criterion. We knew where to go to experience such things – which galleries to visit and which books to read. Painting was the central point of attention. Increasingly social analysis took over from style analysis, but the subject of attention remained for the most part the kind of arti-facts held in the 'temples' of art. Design historians looked at objects that combine overt style or stylishness with functionality. They were concerned with designers as creative individuals and with processes of making, distribution and use. Anthro-pologists, customarily focusing on non-western cultures, tended to deal with the role of object within belief systems and rituals. Historians of various kinds – politi-cal, social, economic, scientific, literary, musical etc – used visual images for a range of illustrative purposes, as part of their evidence or as a general visual ambience for their studies. The corralling worked against any coherent view of how the visual mi-ght have worked holistically in any given culture or in part of that culture. ¶ The need to break down the fences between the corrals has been increasingly acknowl-edged, but genuine crossing of the boundaries is easier said than done, given the over-specialisation that characterises western educational systems to greater or lesser degrees. In the worlds of academia and museums, stock classifications obsti-nately prevail for reasons that are both historical and territorial. Obviously it is not feasible to achieve in the short term the holistic vision that might replace the frag-mented pictures we now have. And that holistic vision will be based on varied com-binations of components in different cultures. There is no universal formula. The best we can presently do is to gain a sense of how such a vision might operate, tak-ing (as happens in modern physics) a particular close-up of a phenomenon as pro-viding a microcosmic view of the whole. Or we might draw an analogy with a holo-gram, in which a fragment of the plate can serve to reconstitute the complete 3-dimensional image. ¶ My personal fragment of the hologram has dealt particularly with the relationship of imagery in art and science, especially with those images that speak of shared intuitions of deeper structures lying beneath appearance. Like all choices of subjects for study, various interlocking factors are involved. My training in both natural sciences and art history is an important part in my personal choice. I have also come to see that the failure of dialogue between the arts and sciences is intellectually and socially disastrous. And there is the personal, instinctive element – the fascination I felt as a child by the shapely drawings in my copy of the Pied Piper (with its multitudinous rats in snaking regiments), the closely packed form of a pine-cone, the spiralling gurgle of water in the bath or the leaping flame in a coal fire. In a sense, my own most developed academic work strives to retain the child's non-compartmentalised innocence about the look of things, untrammelled by whether we think the phenomena belong to art, natural history, chemistry or physics or whatever … ¶ The running thematic motif that has emerged over the years involves what I have called structural intuitions. By this I intend to signal those instincts that lead us to infer an underlying pattern or order beneath the manifold of appearance when we look at a particular feature or process in nature – and, most especially, at the patterns or orders that seem to be shared by otherwise diverse phenomena. The structures to which I refer are thus those embedded in nature, both dynamic and static. But I am also wishing to allude to those cognitive structures with which we are endowed and which resonate with the orders of nature. These cognitive structures are those that enable us to extract functionally effective order from the chaos of sensory inputs. They are, to my mind, both innate and acquired, their potential realised and shaped by our immersion in our environment, particularly during our years of infancy and childhood. The process of interaction between the inner and outer structures is one of mental making and matching. What I am advocating is a type of actively shaped cognition in which our concepts work in a non-arbitrary way with real forms and functions in nature, not a form of Kantian imposition of mental order on outer things. I believe that certain kinds of art and certain forms of science start from this process of ebb and flow in structural intuition. ¶ What this strategy entails is looking at visual characteristics that not only cross disciplines but also cross cultures and eras. It is in the first instance adapted to picking up continuities in our habits of mind. These continuities might be seen as prone to conceal what is specific to local times and places, that is to say to those aspects of a work that embed it in its history. However, I see the strategy as possessing a potential that inverts this seemingly a-historical character. It is when a common core is shaped into particular configurations that the 'accidents' of time and place become most obvious – by systematic comparison. It is rather like comparing a sequence of Renaissance Madonnas. Or an even better example would be a series of scissors produced over the centuries from different geographical areas. The basic function remains unchanged, dictating some basic commonalities of form, while the 'style' speaks of the specifics of time and place through the vehicle of the makers, designers and users of the scissors … ¶ It is within such sequences of related things that the shared elements (like a control in a scientific experiment) allow the variants to stand out most securely. If the basic cognitive elements in structural intuitions are enduring, their realisation in material form is historically specific. Indeed, a particular realisation will not be possible at all times and will only arise in particular cultural, social, economic and material conditions …

Prepared for Radio 3 Nightwaves in September 2006 in response to a request to say who influenced me as a writer

As a student of the Natural Sciences at Cambridge, I spent my summers as a gardener – not much money, but it was pleasant and reasonably creative. My constant companion was a Roberts portable radio – wooden and more than a bit battered. Heaven was pruning roses while listening to ball-by-ball cricket commentaries on the Test Matches. Listening to Wes Hall and Charlie Griffith pounding in and scuttling nervous batmen. Hoping, of course, that Freddie Trueman and Brian Statham would eventually enact revenge.   ¶   Cricket is a game that allows plenty of spaces for words, and its protracted nature lends itself to thoughtful writing. It has attracted writers of an exceptional calibre, including the great West Indian, C L R James. The best of the radio commentators were master of words – real virtuosi, perhaps granted inadequate recognition.   ¶   They painted vivid pictures of the scene – the passing buses, the cluster of pigeons scattered by a raking cover drive, the mood of the crowd, and, above all, the main actors in the fluctuating drama played out of the green stage. And, of course, there were the interruptions due to rain – filled with apparent ease.   ¶   The commentators became my friends. A few words were enough to recognise them – the timbre of the voices, their turns of phrase, their vocabularies, their personalities.   ¶   Above all, there was the masterly John Arlott. As a friend and supporter of Dylan Thomas and aficionado of poetry, his business was words.   ¶   His soft, Hampshire burr seemed warm, comfortable and relaxed, yet he captured everything with razor-sharp incisiveness.   ¶   He was the master of description. He painted the picture, but it was more than this. He captured the tenor of the events, their ebb and flow. And, above all, he snared the personalities, the inner and outer persons. He was a kind of physiognomist of the theatre of cricket. He revelled in the extroverts, yet was able to evoke the dogged character of a stubborn introvert.   ¶   There are a number of Arlott classics. One I particularly treasure is his description of the Pakistani bowler, Asif Masood. Masood ran to the wicket with characteristically loping stride. ¶ 'Here comes Masood into bowl,' Arlott announces. 'Like Groucho Marks chasing a pretty waitress.' It was all there. The lurching gait, eyes focussed remorselessly on the desired goal. Nothing more was needed. Economical yet rich in imagery. ¶ Once play was interrupted by a streaker. Arlott's commentary ran: 'We've got a freaker [with an F] down the wicket now, not very shapely as it is masculine, and I would think it has seen the last of its cricket for the day ... he is being embraced by a blond policeman and this may well be his last public appearance – but what a splendid one!' ¶ What I was absorbing, without knowing it, was a way of using a few words to seduce us into becoming viewers of unseen events. Knowing how little to do is as important as knowing how much. It was a taste that I brought to my reading of the great critics – probably increasingly as I grow older. I fear that I began in a more baroque way that too often betrayed these principles. But I've always got a particular kick from artists who are masters of economy in suggestion. ¶ Vermeer and Chardin are the supreme masters of this – as was Hitchcock in *Psycho*. If you cajole the spectator or the reader into doing much of the work, how much more effectively will something be seen and felt. We think that Vermeer and Chardin offer a lot of detail. They don't. They trigger enough of our perceptual habits to make us do the rest for them – seeing shiny brass where none is really described, or projecting the weave of cloth in an apparently flat patch of paint. ¶ The trick for the writer is to construct a scaffolding of words that describes just enough to suggest much more. It involves the telling phrase that captures our imagination. Kenneth Clark on the Mona Lisa accomplished just this. Clark, like myself, was privileged to have encountered 'her' out of her frame. 'The surface,' he wrote, 'has the delicacy of a new-laid egg and yet it is alive.' That's just right. ¶ Art is a field for interpretation, circumscribed by the rules of its own defining. Cricket, in the hands of Arlott, was just like that.

Like Geese

Walking in the park of autumn,
Leaves of beech copper-gold,
Rustling dry as old bank notes
Clinging to the skeletal branches.
A final declamation of their passing display
In the face of dogged evergreens
Resistant to season and year.

Unseen shots pump from distant shotguns,
Echoing bluntly across the mirrored lake.
Fluttering pheasants, tender in iridescent glory
Tumble limp and folded from the steel grey sky
Towards the eager jaws of favoured hounds.
Geese graze cropped grass
Complacent in the slaughter of those who are not of their kind.

Space Time

I'm craving space, Leonardo's 'continuous quantity.'
Space to breathe the country air,
To hear the distant sounds of stirring nature,
To have no task to perform other than to feel time passing,
Transcendently calm in one of those moments of shared love,
Extending into the geometry of the eternally infinite.

But the jolting assault of the next thing, the next thing, the next thing.
The abrupt, broken discords of outer demands,
The fragmentation of days, hours, minutes, seconds
Into discontinuous shards of numbered events.
Cracked vessels seeping desperate hopes.
Were they ever whole?
Or were they made incomplete,
Mocking illusions of an intactness that never was?

The Shortest Day

Insistent winds hissing in desiccated grasses,
rinsing any hint of comfort from the brittle sun,
all light and no heat.
Tender shoots, wise from eons of experience,
remain invisibly indeterminate like Schrödinger's cat,
both dead and alive,
until we expect
the door of spring to swing open,
arduous months hence.

My shoulders ache,
instinctively hunched around chill ears,
the primitive move of an ancient animal
which knew how to reduce
the ratio of surface area to volume
in distant eras
before geometry was defined in our curriculum.

Our febrile lives
ripple as passing fits
in the circling stasis of what's always happened.

Living seems to me a metaphysical mistake on the part of matter.

Fernando Pessoa (1888–1935), *The Book of Disquiet*, trs. Margaret Jull Costa, 2002, p.114